Dog Tales
for the HEART

Stories of hope, love and wisdom

Edited By Sue A. Hershkowitz, CSP

Dog Tales For The Heart
Stories of hope, love and wisdom

Edited by
Sue A. Hershkowitz

Published by:
High Impact Publications
a subsidiary of High Impact Presentations
Scottsdale, AZ 85254

Printed in the United States of America
Cover design and layout by
Ad Graphics — 800/368-6196
Library of Congress: 95-082109
ISBN: 0-9648464-1-1

To order more copies of this book, or to receive a complete catalog of Sue's products including information on her professional speaking and consultation services please call:

V. 602 996-8864
F. 602 996-6667
E-mail AOL: Hershk
Compuserve:74117,56

To my son, Michael,
and his "brother,"
Champion,
the English Springer Spaniel

For everything you've both
taught me about life

Table of Contents

Acknowledgments 7

Introduction 11

Great Dane-ger 15

Making a Point 19

The Healer 21

Guardian Helper 25

Lost and Found 27

The Mutt 31

And Now...Sports Fans! 35

The Investment 37

The Nature of Love 41

Clear Choices 45

A Proper Good-bye 49

Obedience Training 55

The St. Bernard 57

Faith 61

Of Lice and Men 65

Conditioning 66

The Chicken Caper 69

The Consultant 71

Emergency Rescue 75

The Medical Dog-ter 79

The Big Adventure 83

Friends 87

Love Takes Time 91

Moon Signs 95

Parenting 97

Family *99*

Hair Today, Doggone Tomorrow *103*

Private Lessons *107*

The Dream *111*

The Babysitter *115*

The Boomerang Basset *119*

Proud Mama *125*

Hard Lessons *127*

Royal K-9 .... *131*

Dinner Time *133*

Tennis Anyone? *137*

Only A Dog *139*

Special Delivery *143*

Takin' Care of Grandma *147*

Cute As A Button *151*

Sweet Partings *155*

Instinct *157*

Special Privileges *161*

Memories *163*

Elvis *165*

The Fisherdog *169*

The Business Trip *173*

Doggie Tails *177*

Angels *179*

Fraternity Brothers *183*

Alpha Dog *187*

Thank you! *195*

Who is Sue A. Hershkowitz? *197*

Contributors *199*

Acknowledgments

Dog Tales for the Heart. Why? Because one day I realized that my dog had changed me as a person; he had changed the way I looked at life and had, in fact, changed my life. And as I spoke to friends, colleagues and even strangers on airplanes, I realized that I wasn't the only one crazy enough to not only talk to my dog, but talk for him. I realized I wasn't the only one who felt comforted and calmed by the presence of a companion who happens to be a pet. And I realized that surely I wasn't the only one who thought her dog was the smartest, cutest, most beautiful pet in the whole wide world!

How does one go about gathering hundreds of stories about dogs to select enough to appeal to readers old and young and in-between, readers who are healthy, happy and successful and those feeling more than a bit challenged by circumstances and overwhelmed by obstacles?

You go to your friends. I appealed to 1600 members of the National Speakers Association, my colleagues in the world of professional speaking. Accustomed as we are to revealing ourselves from the platform, I knew I could depend on them to come through. And they did. You'll recognize many famous and soon to be famous names in this book.

And to be certain I would have enough variation, I placed a message on MPINet, the electronic bulletin board of my colleagues within the meeting planning industry. Again, they responded with love, authenticity and integrity.

Friends told friends about the book.. and the stories poured in. Not every submission could be translated for everyone - sometimes you just had to be there. It was difficult to leave those out, however, because in every story you could feel the depth of love and caring for that special pet.

It came together with the very wonderful gift of Evangeline Ysmael, my friend and editor, who could pull out the golden threads when I couldn't. Thank you.

And to Paula Wigboldy, my coordinator and office administrator, who kept it all together while I was simultaneously publishing two books, running a business, speaking on the road, and juggling a family. Paula juggled too and I thank her, and her family, for remembering (and reminding me) that the red dots are what's really important.

And of course, to my family, for the support, love and encouragement for an idea whose time had come.

Sue A. Hershkowitz, CSP
Scottsdale, AZ

Introduction

"Dear Lord,
Please help me to be
half as good a person
as my dog thinks I am!"
Cavett Robert,
Chairman Emeritus -
National Speakers Association

Wouldn't it be wonderful? Wouldn't it be an unbelievable world if everyone would love us unconditionally and simply accept us for what we are - no matter what the imperfection du jour happened to be. Wouldn't it be delightful if we could actually be as good, as kind and as important as our dogs think we are? Ah, what an ideal world!

In fact, it's not like that at all. We live in a world where we often put on a happy face yet feel anything but happy and self assured inside. We live in a place where intimacy has broken down, families are splintered and friendships are transient.

Technology is spinning out of control and it is now more possible than ever to have a greater number of important possessions than (important) friends. Loneliness, heart attacks, and stress related disabilities are rampant.

Our pets are our natural therapists. With no ability to cover up their needs and desires, they love and receive love without condition. Because of this, they have not only come to be a person's best friend, they have also come to the rescue as our doctors and lovers and healers and confidants. They offer us constancy in a world that is ever changing and comfort when others are indifferent. They are our stress relievers, our extended family, and maybe, sometimes our only reason for living. They bring joy to those of us alone, and are anchors of security to those hurting and afraid.

For years, dogs have guided the blind, provided arms and legs for the physically challenged, and interpreted the world for the deaf. Unlike any other animal, our dogs heal our hearts, lick our wounds and make us feel like conquering heroes when they welcome us back to our personal castles.

Research as early as 1972 suggests that dogs help alleviate alienation and loneliness through their friendship and by providing a reason to play and communicate.

More recent studies have demonstrated that a loving relationship with a dog appears to not only help heal sick people, it also seems to make healthy people even healthier. Current research into the therapeutic use of dogs has proven that people who have created a bond with a dog tend to live longer, have fewer heart attacks, get fewer diseases, and when they do get sick, suffer less and get well more quickly.

This book is a love story. It's the love story of each author with his or her dog shared intimately with you, the reader. It's a compilation of personal and true stories designed to inspire readers of all ages to accept and love themselves, and others, unconditionally.

Dog Tales for the Heart is especially designed to cheer the heart and bring joy to the soul. Each story - some funny, some poignant, some routine - when shared, will open lines of communication and help old and young cope more successfully with a world furiously rushing by. The tales offer inspiration, companionship and hope. This book is a gift of love.

"What is man without the beasts? If all the beasts were gone, man would die from great loneliness of spirit."
                              Chief Seatlh, 1855

May you enjoy this gift.

Great Dane-ger

My son, Jack, was married just three weeks ago. The week before the wedding, the young couple packed all their belongings into a truck for their move to the Portland, Oregon area. Jack and Kari, along with Jack's friend Bart, were planning to all live together in a rather large home near Hood River. Bart and Jack drove to Oregon with Bart's gigantic Great Dane puppy, Merlie.

The trip took about four days and Merlie traveled pretty well for being a totally undisciplined puppy. He was huge and unwieldy, but fairly mellow. Merlie was never one to bark or make much noise...

unless someone would say "no" to him. Hearing "no," he'd go berserk barking and prancing around and being generally defiant.

They arrived, unpacked the car, and began hoofing around the grounds looking over their new home. Within an hour of their arrival, Merlie had run like a bat out of hell, not been able to stop at the edge of a cliff, and fallen over a 250 foot cliff. Jack saw him go. When he heard the thud both boys went into absolute mourning. They couldn't see the dog anywhere and the cliff was too steep to scale to search. Merlie was presumed dead. Jack flew home for his wedding a few days hence while Bart stayed to get a bit more composed before flying home for Jack's wedding.

Five days after Merlie's demise and a day before the wedding, a third friend from St. Louis, and his dog, arrived at Bart's doorstep to stay with Bart for a few days while in the area for a rock concert. As Bart began to show Bob the yard, Bob's dog got too near the edge of the cliff. As both boys started to wildly scream "no no no," they heard a familiar answer from the base of the cliff. It was Merlie's usual defiant reply to someone yelling "no."

The boys drove to the bottom of the cliff. Bob, miraculously, a mountain climber climbed the cliff from the base and found Merlie. He had fallen 80 feet onto a ledge that was hidden from view. For over a week, he had been trapped on that tiny ledge. He had some gashes and bruises and had lost quite a bit of weight, but Merlie was still alive! They carried the dog back down the cliff, digging into the steep cliff, and totally exhausted. They were able to get Merlie to a vet, where he stayed for several days before going back to his new home.

Patsy Hall

Making a Point

My partner in the radio business, Jimmy Joe Woodard, loved dogs. Especially bird dogs. Joe was known for having the best bird dogs in our part of the country. One of his very best was ol' Jake. For his birthday one year, Joe's wife hired a photographer to produce a portrait of Jake in point. It was a large, beautiful picture and Joe placed it on the most prominent wall in his spacious office.

Like people, dogs respond to care and attention. Joe fed 'em, played with 'em, trained 'em, worked 'em, and even took 'em swimming. He'd had dozens of 'em. And over the years, two of his favorites were a pair of pointers he named Dot and Zell.

He loved 'em so, when Dot's hips were ruined by arthritis, he spent a handsome sum of money on hip replacement surgery for her.

Of course, a bird dog's job is to point birds, and the good ones live to do it and love to do it, just like the people who are good at what they do. When they spot birds, they lock into a point. And, if they spot another dog in point, they back the other dog by freezing in position and point the other dog. It's a real picture of how teamwork is supposed to be.

After Dot's hips were replaced, her hunting days were over. She became Joe's beloved pet. He'd ride her around with him in his truck during his off time, and she'd follow him wherever he would go.

The first time he brought her to the office, she padded down the hall after him. As she rounded the corner into his office she spotted that portrait of Jake. Dot locked into a magnificent point, right there in the radio station! She was still backing up ol' Jake!

Bryan Townsend

The Healer

It had been a tough year for my father. He had laid to rest a brother, a sister, and a best friend. Another tragedy in the later fall, the suicide of his only son, my brother, was almost more than he could endure. As his youngest daughter, I watched his health deteriorate...an ulcer, hiatal hernia, high blood pressure, heart trouble...the list went on. The thought of losing dad was more than I could bear.

I remembered reading somewhere that older people responded positively, both physically and emotionally, to pets that were brought into the nursing homes. What a great idea! I would give Mom and Dad a puppy for Christmas. I immediately began the search. One evening, my family and I were looking at brand new Poodle puppies. There were four, cute, cuddly, auburn red balls of fur. We each had one in our arms. The one I was holding, snuggled up by my neck, licked my cheek, and laid his head on my shoulder. I was convinced *this* was the dog for my Dad. We left him with his breeder until we could pick him up on Christmas Eve.

My parents came early that December. I picked up the little poodle puppy Christmas eve. Knowing it would be a challenge to keep his presence a secret until Christmas morning when we traditionally opened gifts, I hid him in the bathroom off of my bedroom. And then I kept Dad and Mom from having any reason to be in my bedroom. I wrapped a box and lid in beautiful, festive paper. It was big enough for our surprise puppy gift. I spent most of the night holding the new puppy to keep him from crying and giving away our surprise. Christmas morning, I put him in the beautifully wrapped box, placed the lid on carefully and slipped the box under the tree. I made sure that box was the first gift handed out! I certainly didn't want to suffocate its precious contents!

I handed the box to Mom and she put it back down almost immediately. She pushed it to Dad and said, "Here, it's all yours...it's moving!" Dad took off the lid. It was amazing! As if on cue, the puppy laid his chin on the edge of the box and looked up. His big, brown, puppy dog eyes met Dad's. That was it! It was all over for Dad; he loved him already. Mom was not exactly smitten. "What are we going to do with a dog? We can't keep him. I'm not training a puppy again. He'll ruin our house. How will we get him home?" I showed her both his carrying case - and his airline ticket back to their home. What could she say?

Dad named him Rusty. And the rest of the story, as Paul Harvey would say, is what amazed all of us looking on.

In a matter of two months, Dad's ulcer problems had subsided. So had the indigestion problems and the hiatal hernia. Even more surprising, his blood pressure was back to normal and his heart condition under control. The doctors were amazed. I wasn't. I knew exactly what had happened.

Rusty, a cute, little, red poodle, had jumped into Dad's life, filled it with unconditional love and helped heal the pain of loss. Many times I saw Dad holding Rusty in his lap with Rusty's head nestled in Dad's shoulder. (Who was comforting who?) I was amazed at Rusty's sensitivity. Unlike some French Poodles, nervousness was not in his character, and he never barked. He was calm, loving, and intuitive.

Seven years later, Dad had a heart attack and was placed in intensive care in the hospital. We knew Dad's days were numbered. My oldest son, Jeff, arrived at the hospital one evening sporting an overstuffed Parka. He walked directly into the ICU to visit his grandpa. He closed the doors to the room and slowly unzipped his parka. We watched Rusty climb carefully up the bed and lie his head on Dad's shoulder, lick his cheek, and stay there quietly while they said their last good-byes.

Suzanne Vaughan

Guardian Helper

We are great fans of black Labradors and were fortunate to have had a wonderful Lab we named Shaney of Ellingwood. Shaney lived 15 years before we lost her to cancer.

During her lifetime, she gave us many, many hours of pleasure and on one occasion proved beyond a shadow of a doubt that she was intelligent to boot and knew how to take care of a human!

I can be absent-minded at times, especially when I am focusing on something else and tend to mundane tasks without my mind being truly there. (Am I the only one?)

On this particular occasion, I decided to cook an omelet. I mixed it up, got the pan ready with the fat which needed to be heated. I put the pan with the fat in it on the stove and put the element on high.

Just then, I noticed my laundry sitting in the basket waiting to be hung on the line outside. Always ready to do two things (or more) at once, I figured I would do this quickly and finish making my omelet. Once outside, I was quickly sidetracked, forgetting about the pan on the stove. I was happily hanging the laundry, thinking of the beautiful day and the other things I needed to accomplish that morning. My back was to the door of the house.

I must had been outside for about 10 minutes when I heard the dog yelping and barking behind me.

Toxic, blue smoke was pouring out from the kitchen and Shaney wanted me to pay attention!!! Without her warning, the house would have quickly caught fire. Good thing someone was watching over me!

Joy Fox

Lost and Found

A few years ago, I bought a beautiful small poodle for my daughter. The dog was supposed to live with my daughter and her mother (since I am divorced). I didn't know that her mother had an allergy and couldn't keep the dog. My daughter Caroline was devastated. She pleaded with me to keep the dog in my house and she could visit him whenever she visited me. Well, I am very allergic to dogs myself and my doctor said I couldn't keep a dog in my house. It could kill me. There was only one other alternative I had to try. My parents. I took the poodle in a shopping bag and went to my parents and went inside the house with the dog inside the bag. I asked my mother and pleaded with her in my daughter's name. She finally said yes even though my dad wouldn't like the idea. She asked when I would bring the dog and I handed her the bag!

A few years go by and my dad got to love the dog to the point where he was the only one that took care of him. He fed the animal, took him for walks. He even played ball with him in the back yard. It was really amazing to see that happening since my Dad had never like having animals in the house.

One day, the dog got lost. My parents were very very sad and no one would dare tell Caroline. My father said not to lose hope. He took the car and started looking for the dog all over the neighborhood. He couldn't find him. He then decided to post notices on the light poles offering a $100 reward. A day went by, no dog. He returned to the light poles and changed the notice to $200. Still no dog. The third day he upped the award to $500. He sure wanted to get the dog back. Around 7 PM that night a phone call came in. A lady says she saw the notice and found a dog a couple days ago that matched Mocito's description. My dad said that must be Mocito. The lady says that she likes the dog and wouldn't want to give it away unless it was definitely our dog. She said she wanted proof that he was ours. My dad asked the lady to put the dog on the phone! She comes back to the phone with the dog and says to my father, "OK. I have the dog in my arms." My dad says to put the ear piece on the dog's ear. My dad says, "Mocito, if that is you, BARK!" I swear to God, that dog started barking. The lady got back on the phone and said, "Sir, come and get the dog. It is yours."

My dad picked up the dog and paid the reward. My daughter was never told that Mocito had been lost for a while. Even had she been, I don't know who would have been happiest of all!

Joachim de Posada

The Mutt

The surgeon sat in the den of his fashionable Garden District home with his head in his hands, shaking like the palsy. Sounds that no one had ever heard from him before were escaping—guttural sounds from the soul that one imagines coming from primitive tribes in the Amazon.

But this was Dr. Antoine Giulliand, a prominent New Orleans surgeon I had met through my hospital management work. Antoine's dog had just died. The dog was just a stray mutt, mostly Labrador Retriever, sort of black, certainly not registered. An orphan who parked himself in Antoine's pirouge (Louisiana marsh boat) when he was approximately three months old. Antoine yelled at him, threw mud balls at him, but Buzzard only yelped and refused to leave his seat on Antoine's hunting jacket. That night we fed him scraps, outside, in the miserable weather, not even needing to discuss the fact that he would be left when we headed back to New Orleans in the morning.

The next day, I was awakened by having my face licked good morning. I asked Antoine how the pup had managed to get in. He grumbled and grumped and changed the subject. Then I told him I thought I would do the little bugger a favor and take him to the New Orleans SPCA, for they surely could find him some kind of home. Antoine thanked me but said he knew some people who he just might be able to talk into giving him a home. George, who had been quiet throughout everything (as is his nature), told us both to quit fretting, for if his wife approved, the poor thing could maybe stay with him. (A few years later the three of us recounted this incident and laughed when we realized that Buzzard had licked all of our faces. At the time, however, we each thought we were the chosen one.)

When we were hunting, Antoine never acted like a big shot. His dominant, surgeon's personality disappeared in favor of being one of the guys. But he suddenly loomed seven feet tall on his 5'9" frame! "The frigging dog sat on my frigging hunting coat in my frigging pirouge, so he's my frigging dog. Understand?" We did.

Twelve years later, a man who by the world's standards had everything, suddenly felt he had nothing. A craggy orphan mutt was dead and Dr. Antoine Guilliand's wealth and prestige suddenly seemed meaningless.

Buzzard is securely buried in Antoine's heart now. Nothing can ever take his place. But Buzzard Jr. is romping toward Antoine's outstretched hand with an old, rolled-up sock. Dr. Antoine Guilliand is on his hands and knees, roaring a hearty, gruff laugh, signifying that he is once again alive and someone to be contended with.

Twyman Towery, PhD., FACHE

And Now...
Sports Fans!

I wanted to teach our lively Keeshound named
"Keesha" something a little different than the
usual tricks. She already knew how to "sit" and
"shake hands" and the other standard repertoire.

Being a sports fan, I taught Keesha to bark and spin
in circles when the name of our Indianapolis foot-
ball team, the "Colts" was mentioned. She learned
well. If you say "Packers," "Bears" or "Cowboys,"
she'll just look at you. But mention the Indianapolis "Colts" and she will twist, turn, bark and generally go a little nuts like any good sports fan - and
then wait for her treat.

The one thing I didn't anticipate was a recent dinner party at our home, where a friend of mine — a 6'7", 330 pound linebacker for a certain local team would be in attendance.

When a guest from out of town asked him what he did for a living, he loudly and proudly stated that he played for the "COLTS!" At that instant, Keesha heard her cue. What had been a quiet little dog now was a lunatic. She started barking, spinning in circles and jumping up and down. The linebacker moved quicker in our living room than he ever has on the field. Imagine Keesha's surprise when she quietly sat for her treat and no one was paying attention to her.

We were, instead, looking out the front window at the scared linebacker on the lawn.

Scott McKain

The

Investment

Chelsea is my daughter-in-law Jean's dog. Of course, that makes Chelsea my grandpup. A Weimaraner, she's big for a female and has all the grace of a clumsy reindeer! Chelsea was the apple of her owners' eyes for two years.

Early 1993, two important events occurred. Jean was pregnant with their first child and Chelsea ran into the road and was severely injured by a car. Chelsea's back leg was broken in several places and required an orthopedic surgeon to reconstruct her leg.

The $1000 surgery for Chelsea, a baby due in six weeks, and very limited funds made for an immensely difficult decision. Without the surgery, Chelsea would be crippled. The only alternative was to put her to sleep.

My grandson, Paul III, arrived on January 26, 1993. I found myself helping Jean, caring for my first grandchild and playing nursemaid to a dog recovering from major surgery. Chelsea could walk on only three legs, and needed a great deal of care. She wasn't going to let that stop her from her "rightful" job as "Nanna" in residence.

When Paul would awaken during the night she would hobble in to Jean's room and nudge her awake, lead her into the nursery, sit there sleepily while Paul had his bottle and then slowly and painfully return to her bed.

There are many tales of Chelsea's devotion to little Paul but the one we all remember was the day Chelsea saved Paul's life. Paul had just started crawling. There are some very steep stairs leading down into the basement. Jean always kept that door securely closed. Jean had just walked into another room when she heard a toy with bells in it bouncing down the basement stairs. She flew in panic knowing that the door was somehow open and Paul must be at the top of the stairs about to follow the toy.

When Jean arrived at the door, she found Chelsea standing (as firmly as a dog with three good legs can stand) on the top step, refusing to allow Paul to follow the toy. Paul was laughing as she kept nudging him each time he tried to crawl toward the toy. Paul thought this was a great game as Chelsea stood her ground.

We all agreed later, after everyone stopped shaking, that $1000 was the wisest investment ever made!

Ann Weeks, DNS

The Nature of Love

"That's the way it happens in nature - survival of the fittest," we were told.

"But the mother duck has been chased away and now the crows are attacking the baby ducks," we pleaded. "Their nest is in our yard by the lake and we feel responsible."

"Sorry, we don't interfere with nature," the animal shelter director told us.

"Well, then, we will," said my wife, Lynn. "We won't let those baby ducks be eaten. They don't have a chance against the crows and the neighborhood dogs."

"But Lynn," I questioned, "What about Mele? She's a Golden Retriever, a bird dog! What will *she* do to the baby ducks?"

"We will teach her to love and protect them," Lynn said calmly.

So we did. At first, Mele was curious but not aggressive or jealous when we introduced her to her ducky housemates. We fashioned a nest in the tub in our guest bathroom, allowing the ducks to prepare for release in the lake. For exercise, the ducks went for daily walks in the yard with Mele. The ducks imprinted on Mele and the group became a family.

As summer arrived, as it sometimes does in Seattle, the ducks were ready to take their first swim in the lake. To our surprise, Mele swam right along with them and then she led them back home. At nap time, when Mele would sleep in the grass, the ducks would lie down with - and sometimes - right *on* - her.

The ducks grew larger and began to swim farther. They were staying outside now, but came back to our yard for visits with Mele, their "mom." And then the visits ended.

We will never know if they were victims of "nature's way" or if they survived to become parents themselves. What we do know is that Mele often swims in the lake, as if she were looking for the ducks. Mele still barks at other dogs, but ducks are always welcome in our yard!

Love is learned. *That's* the way it works in nature!

Dr. Stephen Yarnall, MD

Clear Choices

On Labor Day evening our 19 1/2 year old dog, Waggles (who got his name because he wagged his tail so frequently), was in and out and in and out every half hour. With his sight going and his hind legs occasionally giving out on him Helen was surprised how active he was being. "You want to go out again?!" I said after what felt like the fiftieth time that night. It was 10:30 PM and the last time he ever went out because he never returned. We walked the neighborhood calling, whistling and clapping our hands as we went.

Our son, Peter, the dog's best friend, had cleaned his room three weeks previously to this and had left for college. On this Labor Day we decided to "labor" by cleaning our office and throwing much away. We think our dog thought we were going to leave him too and so he decided to go first before we had the chance.

As Helen laid in bed early that morning, unable to sleep, she heard a very loud yelp from a distance and immediately knew it was our dog. She jumped out of bed and moments later the phone rang. The neighbors, two streets away, had our dog. He had been hit by a car that never stopped. After picking Waggles up, he lay almost lifeless in the back seat. We took him to the vet who gave him a shot and said he would see what he could do.

A long hour later we received a call at work; the dog needed tests to determine the extent of the life threatening damage and he would have to have his tail removed. Waggles without a tail? My heart broke as I told them no, I didn't think we would have that done.

As we called each of our eight children, we cried again and again.

Today, years later, there are more tears in our eyes

for Waggles. But we've learned the important things in life never really leave; instead they leave us richer, and more tolerant, kinder and much more wise.

Joe and Helen Hesketh

A Proper Good-bye

This is a love story about Tiki and Heather, who we recently lost to cancer.

Tiki & Heather were Cairn Terrier litter mates that came into my life when they were 7 weeks young. They passed on at ages 13 and 14. I never had two legged children; only the four legged variety.

We drove two hours in 30 degree below chill factor temperatures to select one new pet. With only two pups left, you guessed it, we came home with two - "the girls". The dress-up photo sessions started early on with professional baby pictures taken right away.

Every holiday thereafter, out came the costumes and my roll of film. They truly loved having their pictures taken. They would sit still and pose for half an hour while I dressed them as devils, witches, pumpkins, angels, reindeer, Santa Claus, bunnies, flags, hearts, leprechauns, beach bums and turkeys. (I was urged to publish calendars with "the girls" as monthly centerfolds. I wish now I had.)

They had the best dispositions, better than most people I know! They were always there for me, that unconditional love was more than I could ever imagine. They never left my side if I was sad or sick; they were always there. All the endless crying and fights during my divorce, I couldn't have gotten through it without their love and wet kisses. They would lick my tears away and it would all be better. They may have needed me but I needed them more.

Tiki loved the pool. Frequent swimming caused a horrible ear infection. We tried everything but Tiki lost her hearing. It broke my heart. She had to depend on Heather to be her ears. She could tell by Heather's reactions what was going on. Heather told her when the garage door would open or when it was thundering or if I called them. They were *always* side by side.

One morning a few months later Heather couldn't stand up. I rushed her to the specialist Tiki was seeing and she was diagnosed with a stroke, a week later they thought ulcers, the next week a slipped disc, then suddenly the office Doberman was giving Heather blood to keep her alive. I slept with her on the table round the clock and held her little arm straight for the IV's. I never left her side. We took her to more doctors but it was too late. The cancer had consumed her tiny body. The end happened so fast I didn't even get to say good-bye properly. We all mourned for weeks. Poor Tiki lost her litter mate and her ears, she looked everywhere for Heather. She was so pitiful; we all were. Tiki and I got each other through another bad time.

After awhile, Tiki, receiving all the attention, began to blossom and her entire personality changed. She became very relaxed. I worked out of the house and I started taking her everywhere with me. She even learned sign language. It was amazing. She loved when we made fresh pasta and got all the dropped noodles. She loved bubble baths and the hair dryer. She'd lay forever while I dried and brushed her hair. She was such a snuggler and loved her evening back rubs Allan gave her. She slept on my pillows and snored in my ear and I even got used to it.

Then my worst nightmare came true; Tiki had a heart attack while getting her teeth cleaned. It was the same exact week Heather got sick the year before and it was happening all over again.

My regular vet, Allison (and dear friend) wanted her to see a heart specialist right away. It was Friday and the soonest the specialist would see us was Monday. It couldn't wait. I went to her office and sat in the waiting room holding Tiki for six hours until the doctor finally saw us. It was 8:00 PM and the prognosis was not good. I thought I could deal with heart problems - anything but cancer. All I knew was I did not want her to suffer like Heather did toward the end. She had to be on IV's so Tiki's internist, Susan, took her home with her for the weekend so she could treat her. I was still trying to be optimistic. I didn't realize until later that Susan (a new dear friend) nursed her back to health so I could have a little extra time to say good-bye. I never let Tiki out of my sight. I slept on the floor with her. I fed her with a dropper when necessary. I carried her out and helped her squat to relieve herself. She seemed to be rallying but suddenly got worse and by Wednesday night she couldn't even kiss me. She *never* missed a chance to give kisses. That's when I knew it was her time. She had cancer too. We got through the night together and we took her to Susan's office at 8 am. I didn't want Tiki to see what was going on (she was deaf) so I covered our heads together with her blanket and we got nose to nose breathing together. We just kept petting and kissing her. I couldn't give the signal. Then Tiki's little tongue gave me a slow, strained kiss. She had not even been able to lift her head for the last 12 hours, but she gave me a last kiss. That was the signal. Then she was gone. It was a proper good-bye.

Mauri Way

Obedience Training

Our miniature Poodle, Sweetie Pie, an extremely bright, easy to train animal, loved to please and did a number of fun tricks. One of her tricks was to jump up on the fire hydrant located in our front lawn, curl up comfortably and watch as my husband Len mowed the lawn.

One Sunday just as Len was completing the lawn the phone rang. It was his sister calling long distance. Len quickly came in, talked with his sister and then sat down with the family for dinner. Half way through dinner, we got another phone call. This time it was our neighbor. "Have you forgotten that

Sweetie Pie is still sitting on the fire hydrant?" she asked.

Now that's a well trained pooch. Our children, I'm sorry to say, were never quite as obedient.

Elaine Kvitka

The
St. Bernard

My eyesight is severely diminished. I have retinitis pigmentosa in which I gradually lose my peripheral vision. Three years ago I stopped driving when I hit a building that I didn't see. (Hey, but guess what, *I don't have to drive*!!!) I use a cane in unfamiliar settings and in crowds, mostly to indicate to other people I don't see well. In familiar settings, I manage quite well thank-you-very-much. That's why I can walk all over the neighborhood and in the surrounding country side without a cane. I know the territory. But, I do feel somewhat vulnerable and I must work hard at seeing which is how Noah came to live with us.

I may need a seeing eye dog in the future, but I've never had a dog of my own, only family dogs, so I was interested in being around a dog *before* I need one. Although I claimed the dog was for our two young sons, I knew this dog would be for me.

We found Noah, our St. Bernard mix, black and white nine-month old, 60 lb. pup at the animal shelter. He was on his back, neck on the ground, front legs folded, back legs spread, lying very, very still, tired from being held by everyone who thought he was so cute, but who didn't want a big hairy dog in their home in the South in the summer.

The eyes of the volunteer brightened when we told her what kind of a dog we were looking for. Then, we saw him, lying there. Anybody will tell you to select a dog with personality and curiosity. Noah just lay there. We gathered him up, placed him in our collective laps and stroked him. Noah's legs dangled as my younger son picked him up and hugged Noah's chest to his. We walked around to inspect the other dogs and cats there. But Noah was the one. The manager/volunteer told us those dogs are frequently returned to the shelter in June and July. She tried hard to talk us out of taking him, concerned we, too, would return him. I knew he was right for us.

My husband was out of town when we brought Noah home. I had told him before he left that we may have a dog when he returned. He protested, but it was three to one. As the boys played with him in the front yard, I left a message, "Kirk, you're a daddy again." He called back and asked what kind of dog it was and I told him. *"St. Bernard*!!!!!" he shouted. I pulled the phone away from my ear and calmly said, "We don't know for sure." Of course, the boys were telling everyone they could, "Our dog is half St. Bernard," and I was shushing them as fast as I could.

That was six months ago, and yes, he's hot, he slobbers, and he's big, but he sees, hears, loves and fills a gap we didn't know we had. He, like my cane, brings out the best in people. We'll keep him!

Ann Humphries

Faith

Tashi, our Lhasa Apso, was not one to stray from our unfenced yard. When he turned up missing one day, it alarmed us since several cases of dogs being stolen had been reported in our neighborhood. He was a friendly type with more bark than bite and would not have resisted any "dognapping" attempt.

After many trips through the neighborhood calling him, using our familiar whistle that he always responded to, and looking in every conceivable place, he was not to be found. We made lost dog signs and placed them on utility poles listing his description and our phone number.

My wife, Lynn, was leading a weekly Bible study for teenagers in our home and she shared our loss with the group. During a prayer, one of the young-sters asked for Tashi to be found and returned.

Weeks passed without any trace of our beloved pet. But each week, the teenagers continued to pray for his return. There were a few calls from neighbors who thought they had seen him but each report proved unsuccessful.

After six weeks, we decided to remove the signs. We were convinced that Tashi had probably become a victim of dog snatching. All the signs were re-moved except one. It was at a busy intersection where heavy traffic made it rather difficult to re-trieve. It was easier just to leave it there.

On the morning of July 5th, the phone rang. A woman, who resided some five miles away, was call-ing to explain that while Fourth of July fireworks were exploding near her house, a frightened little dog ran toward her. He appeared lost and disori-ented. She opened the back yard gate and gave him food and water.

While driving through that intersection the following morning, she noticed our last remaining sign. The description fit the dog in her back yard, so she wrote down the phone number and called.

Lynn's initial reaction was that it was another false lead. But, like all the others, she would check it out. She drove to the address, walked into the back yard where a dirty, hair-matted, smelly dog saw her and came running with his tail wagging. There was no doubt, Tashi had been found.

How he disappeared and what he experienced in those many weeks remain a mystery. But the power of faith and prayer came vividly clear in that tearful reunion.

Gene Swindell

Of Lice and Men

I 've always thought people who made a big fuss about their animals were ridiculous.

Then we got Rocky and that beautiful, noble dog lived with us for 14 years. Now my opinion is different. There isn't a time I see a German Shepherd, I don't think of her and miss her and get a lump in my throat. I wish I hadn't worried so much about her shedding in my clean house.

We do so much talking and planning about sweeping social reforms. Files bulge with notes and recommendations for correcting biases — just as it did with Rocky and me. I love dogs now. I wonder why I'm comparing people to dogs?

Perhaps because I feel we could learn a lot from them.

§§§§§§§§§§§§§§§§§§§§§§

Conditioning

She was just a mutt and would never take Rocky's place. I let her know that from the beginning. I fed her and put fresh water in her dish but that was about it. One day she would not eat. Or the second. Or the third. I patted her and stroked her and asked her what was wrong. The caring in my voice surprised me. She gobbled up the food, drank the water, and wagged her tail. Weeks later I was convinced it was a coincidence based on other variables. She could have been ill. (I was taught to be objective in school.)

So I just put the food out without petting her first. By the second day of not eating, the experiment was complete and I needed no other proof.

If a pat on the head can mean that much to a dog,
can you imagine what a hug must mean to a child?

Rosita Perez
From: The Music Is You
(With Permission)

The
Chicken Caper

B randy, our toy poodle, must have understood the importance of goals because she was sure focused. Her goal and mission? Seek out and retrieve all and any food products, especially if it wasn't really meant for her consumption! And because she was so clever, she usually succeeded in achieving her goal! (Amazingly, she never had a weight problem. I suppose it was a result of the effort she expended during her search and seizure activities.)

Most of us have pushed the fridge door closed and walked away thinking it had latched properly only to discover later it was still ajar. This was the case one afternoon when I had placed a ten piece box of fried chicken on the lower shelf and returned to work after lunch.

That evening when I got home I found Brandy in my bedroom very glad to see me. She rushed into my bathroom and begged for water. I picked her up to say *hello* thinking she felt *very heavy* and I was amazed at the amount of water she gulped down. (These may be things you notice only as the owner of a small dog.) I had that strange nagging feeling that something was amiss.

After slipping off my shoes and hose, Brandy and I set off to the kitchen. In the middle of the floor was an empty box. No bones, no crumbs. No evidence except for the perfectly empty box!

Luckily, she didn't suffer any ill effects from the bones; but the grease and spices played havoc with her system for a week in spite of a visit to the vet. She recovered, lived eight more years (to a ripe old age of 15) and went on to learn the fine art of opening lower kitchen cabinets to confiscate items in the trash. Getting in was easy, getting out wasn't. But that's another story.

Mary Pennington

The Consultant

My dog Toku is a six year old black and white female Akita, with a high sensitivity to people. Toku is generally more comfortable with women than men. Yet she still discriminates in favor of those who give off good vibes.

When I put an ad in the local paper for an office administrator, two applicants responded. I interviewed both and chose the woman with 10 years office experience (we'll call her Betty) over the recently married woman who had put aspirations on hold to be a TV anchor woman. I hired Betty over Toku's protest. She did not like Betty from the beginning, growled and was uneasy around her, but warmed immediately to the second applicant. All the early signs of Toku's choice were obvious.

When Betty came to work the first day, Toku barked at her and kept her distance. I thought she was off the mark on this one and ignored her displeasure.

Betty showed up with her own ideas about doing the job. We began every morning with about a half hour of dictation on a book I was writing. At times she just quit taking short hand. When I would ask her why she wasn't writing, she responded that she didn't think that what I was saying was important. I asked her to use the restroom next to her office rather than the bathroom in my living quarters, but she found a reason to enter the living quarters once a day. I asked her not to use my Mont Blanc pen. She wrote me notes with it. And her typing was so bad that I would spend good time retyping envelopes and labels to correct mistakes after she had left for the day.

After Betty's first few days, when she would come to work in the morning, Toku started to bark as soon as she heard the car pull up in front of the house. This was a response usually reserved for the garbage truck, not for a woman in a Ford Tempo. But Betty was starting to irritate me too; and frankly, I felt like barking right along with Toku.

Betty and I had a peaceful parting. When I gave her notice, she had already found a full-time job. However, over the next few months I found a disproportionate number of my management books that she had sent out on approval to potential buyers, had not arrived. This all happened only during Betty's brief tenure.

Toku's response to job applicants is now a major consideration in my selection process. Who says you can't find a good consultant right in your own backyard!

Paul Radde

Emergency Rescue

Never one to watch much television, I grimaced when Michael, my nine year old son kept badgering me to watch "911 - Police Rescue." "Oh, ma, it's about a dog, come watch." Reluctantly, expecting the dog to die, I sat with him.

The German Shepard on the TV reenactment had swallowed a ball he had been playing with. The dog tried hard to expel it but all he could do was make this odd coughing sound. Just in time, they took the dog to a police substation and wouldn't you know it, it was the station where they train police dogs and the trainer was there and he gave the dog mouth to mouth (sort to speak) and the dog was saved. Nice story.

Two days later, I hear the *identical* coughing sound coming from my Springer Spaniel, Champion. I checked the ball situation and all were accounted for. He wasn't coughing a lot... but it sure was the same sound. Michael noticed it as well. I had some errands to run and when I got back, Champion was still making the sound - and more frequently.

I was scheduled to fly out to a speaking engagement in Denver that night. Because of the 911 show I decided to call the vet and mention the coughing sound to see if she sounded alarmed, concerned or nonchalant about it all. I described the sound and she immediately made room for me to bring him in. A few x-rays later and it was confirmed; something was obstructing Champion's stomach. If it didn't pass by morning, we would have no choice other than surgery.

I left him in her care (crying all the way to the airport). Following her directions, I phoned at exactly 7:45am. "We're preparing Champion now. He hasn't passed anything."

I'm hysterical and I have a presentation in fifteen minutes. With all my might I focused on the audience and delivered my program. Even though I was scheduled to be a panelist later that afternoon, I knew I couldn't stay - no matter what. I explained the situation to the meeting planner trying my best to keep it together. When I started crying, he knew he had to get me to the airport.

We arrived at 11:57 AM for a 12:05 flight. I ran through the terminal and got to the gate to hear "We are in an oversold situation. If you are willing to volunteer your seat..." I didn't even have a reservation! As quickly as I could, I ran to the gate agent, "I have to get on this flight. I have to get home to a sick...(what was I going to say?) baby." I am now absolutely hysterical. "Ma'am, we'll see what we can do." That wasn't good enough.

I decided I had to take things into my own hands. The vet was willing to wait for me past her normal closing hour, but at 4:00 PM she would have to transfer Champ to a pet hospital. I wouldn't be able to see him until Monday morning. I had to do something, fast. I took out my check book and started yelling and waving checks. "I'll pay for your seat..I'll buy your seat..I have to get home to a sick....baby."

The guy behind the ticket counter was embarrassed for me (I would've been too had I been in my right mind!). "Ma'am, if you'll just sit here quietly, we'll get you on the plane." *Yes*!!!

I made it to the vet before she closed .

Apparently Champion had found some house stucco in his archeological digging. In his stomach, the stucco had broken into a bunch of smaller pieces - all loaded with fiberglass. Seventy stitches later my dog was alive and recuperating. And 911 had really come to the rescue.

Sue Hershkowitz

The
Medical Dog-ter

Because I work out of my home, my Newfoundland dog, Molly Bloom, often sits in on the psy-
chotherapy sessions I conduct. It's embarrassing
how she sometimes snores loudly in sessions, or gets
up and walks out when my patients show a lot of
emotion. One day I was working with a couple,
when the wife became very angry and upset. She
was sure her husband and I were somehow in ca-
hoots together and that no one cared about her. She
began crying and yelling, usually a cue for Molly
Bloom to walk out. Instead, Molly ran to the women
and put her big head in the woman's lap. The
woman, sobbing hysterically, started to pet the dog,

saying, "At least you love me Molly." After a while the woman calmed down. From then on I thought Molly a brilliant psychotherapist.

§§§§§§§§§§§§§§§§§§§§§§

Noodles, my female black Labrador puppy, accompanied me everywhere.

It was my first evening as a volunteer support group leader at our local AIDS project and I was a bit worried about how she might behave. I didn't need to worry! She spent that first night going from lap to lap, snuggling and licking each of the participants in my group. I think she gave more support to the group than any one else could have!

Edgar, a close friend who had often baby sat Noodles when I couldn't have her with me, became ill with AIDS. I really wanted to take the dog to visit him after he came home from the hospital, but, again, was concerned about her behavior. In the past Edgar had encouraged Noodles to jump on him and climb into his lap. He would often roughhouse with her and I was afraid she might be a bit too rambunctious. To our surprise when Noodles saw Edgar she gently put her head in Edgar's lap for a few minutes so he could pet her, and then she quietly went to sleep with her head on his foot. "Nurse Noodles" understood the situation perfectly.

Judy Tatelbaum, MSW

The Big Adventure

The gate was open, the hunt was on. Our Shetland Sheepdog, Vegas, saw his chance for a big adventure and took it. He left our fenced-in, half-acre yard for new sights, fresh smells and perhaps a bit of mischief. The trouble was that he was an old dog with clouded vision, arthritis, and poor hearing. When my husband and I discovered his yard-break, we feared he was headed for misadventure instead.

During his rare disappearances in the past, he proved that his homing instinct was impaired. We would shout his name as we looked for him and see him jogging around the neighbor's home trying to find us. Now, age had taken its toll and Vegas couldn't hear us nor see any familiar landmarks. And he wasn't wearing tags. We thought (mistakenly) that because he stayed within the back yard or in our home, he didn't need to be encumbered with a set of noisy, uncomfortable dog tags.

We started the search along the perimeter of our neighbors to the north. During his few past outings, we would find him venturing no farther than the next house or two. It wasn't true this time, so we extended the hunt into the neighborhood behind us. No luck and now daylight was gone. We would have to wait to continue until the next day.

In our hearts, we didn't think he would survive the night; it was the first dip below freezing for the season. Trying to be optimistic, and hoping that some kind soul had taken him in, we decided to try a campaign of flyers with Vegas' description and our phone number. Perhaps someone would be generous enough to open their heart to him.

And they did! As a result of the flyers, we received a call from a gentleman who had seen our dog a few blocks north and across the street. We didn't think to look in that area. Vegas had never gone that way before.

Armed with the new information, we distributed additional flyers in the new region. We received more calls, which sent us further north, and with each subsequent caller we added new clues to his whereabouts. With the daylight, we explored the new area, but came away empty-handed. We later learned that a wonderful woman had taken him in to warm him up, but had to let him go again when she left for a meeting. Finally we received the call that we desperately wanted. Based on the flyer's description, a woman said she found Vegas and would be happy to bring him home to us.

The next day we put his dog tags on and kept them on until he died three years later though he never did try to yard break again. We suspect that Vegas' Big Adventure wasn't the thrill that he initially imagined. All of us, however, learned a little more about the generosity of strangers.

Terri Horvath

Friends

The first time I saw Clyde was when he and his litter mates were tearing across the yard and he tripped and started rolling toward me like a little, round fluffy ball. Little did I know that in less than two years Clyde would be hunting the swamps and bayous of Louisiana like a seasoned professional.

A lot of bird dog men make fun of Brittanies, thinking these little critters could never match their wide ranging Setters and Pointers. Clyde, with his splash of orange and white, cropped tale and floppy ears, running through the bush, made a believer out of everyone who observed him. In Tennessee, an old friend and the best bird hunter I've ever roamed the hills with, scoffed at the very idea of a Brittany being able to match his veteran setters. But by the end of our first hunt, my hunting partner was paying attention to Clyde over the other dogs — the greatest compliment my little buddy could have received.

But Clyde's greatest trait was being a wonderful companion to both children and adults. He loved being a member of the family. People who think a dog can't be a rugged hunter and a loving friend both, don't really know dogs. The talented Clyde was dearly loved by all who experienced him.

At seven years old a cruel infection invaded Clyde and we could only watch while he suffered a slow, painful good-bye. My vet called on a dreary Saturday afternoon and said he had taken Clyde outside for a few minutes, where he went into his hunting posture — and died. The space Clyde left in our hearts was unfillable.

The next day, I had to take an early morning flight on a business trip and found myself at the ticket counter crying. Everyone was embarrassed and looked away. Later I was sobbing in the boarding area and people changed seats to avoid me. I upgraded to first class with a frequent flyer coupon and sat alone. Once into the air the tears started flowing and the sobs ripped loose again. A flight attendant stopped, sat down by me, and asked what was wrong. I told her and she told me about her dog who had died almost two years ago. We cried together and held hands. And we both felt better.

Twyman Towery, PhD., FACHE

Love Takes Time

"No," I said for the ninetieth time, "we cannot get a dog. They shed, they track in mud, they need lots of attention, and they're expensive to keep. No and that's final."

But my son was eight and recently survived the break up of my marriage and he cried for a dog. My mistake was going to the pet shop.

There in front of us was the most beautiful, playful puppy I had ever seen. The pet store people said he was a Springer Spaniel and that he had papers - and I had no idea what that meant - did he come with newspapers to be trained on? I had never owned a dog.

We left the shop with the dog, and food, and a bed, and bowls, and toys, and a book, "Everything You Need to Know About Springer Spaniels."

"No, he may not come inside," I said. "He is an animal and you can keep him but if you want to play, you'll have to go outside with him."

I was the one who went outside. Champion (Sir Shmendrick of Scottsdale for those AKC papers!) would sit and look up at me through the glass in the patio door with those large, dark, pathetic Springer eyes. (I know he was wondering why he was exiled to the backyard - after all no one else in the family lived out there!)

When the weather turned a *bit* chilly (we live in Scottsdale, Arizona!), I wedged bricks into the back garage door so he could come into the garage at night and warm up. He looked so sad that I'd leave the light on; that way, he wouldn't be afraid in the dark.

It seemed to get really cold that year in Arizona and

I started letting him in for short bits of time. First, during the day. Then the night.

And when I was recently remarried, I explained in no uncertain words to my new husband, "This is Champion's part of the bed. Don't disturb him when you sleep."

Sue Hershkowitz

Moon Signs

She had been abandoned on a dirt road, with her partner Shadow, for at least eight weeks. We started to feed them about ten days before we brought them home. Her name was Moon. She was a mutt, half Beagle and half Bull Dog. She had an underbite that made her look funny. People told me how ugly she was.

Two days after she started to live with us, I found out that I had a chronic illness. The first few days, I sat outside with tears streaming down my face. She knew I was sad and did everything she could to take care of me.

About three months after Moon and Shadow became family members, we had to put Shadow to sleep. She was a wild dog who was killing the farmer's chickens. The sheriff said the only life she could have was to be on a chain. We couldn't do that to a wild dog! The decision was hard, but it had to be made.

We buried Shadow that evening near our house. The next day I heard a whimper at my office door. I opened the door to hear Moon crying. She came in and we sat down on the floor and cried together.

From that moment on, Moon never left my side. Without her, my life would not be the same. To some she might be ugly, to me she is the most beautiful animal in the world.

Margot Robinson

Parenting

When we adopted her, her name was "Queenie." We decided to give her a few days to live with us to determine "who" she really was. After seeing her playful spirit, her ability to leap to great heights, we anointed her "Jumper." She greets all our friends by jumping into their lap (which isn't exactly what they expect from a mid-sized dog!). Instead of playing catch like most dogs, she'd rather jump for her "pull-toy."

Jumper spends a great deal of her time learning from her friends on the other side of the fence. Floppy and Deuce are the two over-fed long ear neighbor bunnies. Jumper greets them each morning and "communicates" with them throughout the day. There are constantly new holes in the wooden fence that grow as the conversations get more intense.

Convinced that she should spend more time with the children doing "dog" things, we try to encourage her to play catch. She's learning. The fact that she runs two steps, leaps, runs two more steps, and leaps to the Frisbee brings us continuously back to our parenting role. It's true with dogs and children. You cannot not model!

Paula Wigboldy

Family

My wife Linda's Lab mix, Tootie (named after the girl on *Facts Of Life*) was with her since she was a puppy. More widely traveled than most dogs, she lived with Linda in Kansas, Missouri, New York and Maine. When Linda moved to Calgary, Canada in 1988 to share her life with me, Tootie came along - Love me, love my dog. Tootie was already 10 years old but adapted well and loved going with us to a big field where she was sure some day she would actually catch one of the gophers she chased.

Thinking it would be nice for Tootie to have a companion we looked for a second dog. After introducing her to three dogs, on three different occasions, at the SPCA, she finally accepted Buster, a year-old stray Poodle mix. They played together, ate out of each other's food bowl and often slept together with Buster curled up against Tootie.

A year later, I agreed to take a dog my son had in North Carolina. They were moving to Iowa and their new apartment complex didn't allow dogs. Our newest family member was a two-year-old, 90-pound Rottweiler, Toby, who is sure he is a lap dog. Based on his personality, we nicknamed him Bubba.

Bubba and Buster got along great. Tootie and Buster got along great. But Tootie wanted nothing to do with Bubba and the feeling was mutual. They tolerated each other but had the occasional lip curled, snarling, snapping confrontation. And this is what makes the story interesting.

By November of last year, Tootie had reached the point where she had lost most of her strength. There was no play left in her, she had no appetite and, for the most part, she was ignored by the other two dogs who now played with each other. I had to carry her upstairs at night and back down in the morning. She was not even able to navigate the two steps leading from the deck, where the dog door was located and had to be carried out and back for calls of nature.

One morning while working in my office, which overlooked the back yard, I heard Bubba barking. A few minutes later Buster joined in. Thinking they were playing, or that someone was crossing the park in back of the house, and smiling at the sound of a soprano and bass barking duet, I ignored it. When it continued non-stop, I opened the window and yelled at them.

They now barked louder and with a sound I had never heard coming from either of them. I looked out the window and saw Tootie laying spread-eagled on the snow in front of the steps. She had some-how managed to get down the steps but was too weak to make it back up, or even to stand up. Her "brothers" who had ignored her for weeks, were sounding the alarm and were not about to stop un-til somebody paid attention.

I went down, picked Tootie up, and carried her in-side. We knew that day we could no longer delay the inevitable. On November 26, 1994, with Linda holding her on the table and me looking her in the eyes and talking to her, we allowed Dr. Larson to euthanize her.

Bubba and Buster will never be Lassie. But that one day they were our heroes.

Dick Caldwell

Hair Today,
Doggone Tomorrow

O ne of my favorite practical jokes was pulled off using only my imagination and my dog Freeway. A client called me on a Saturday morning. She was frantic because she had forgotten her best friend's birthday and had to have something crazy delivered right away. I asked her for background information on the birthday boy. He owned an exclusive hair salon and he'd be there until two o'clock.

The pressure was on. What can I do in a hurry that is related to hair? About that time Freeway started barking. As I let him out, I noticed he had a few patches of missing hair. The idea hit me then.

My client loved it. I hid balloons in my trunk and told Freeway it was time for him to earn his keep. I told him he owed me a lot for all the dog food and jerky treats I had bestowed upon him over the years. He reluctantly agreed.

We showed up at the hair salon where the owner's white Rolls Royce was parked out front. I put Freeway on a leash, and barged right into the Salon.

I demanded to see the owner. The receptionist told me in an uppity tone, "Take that 'dog' out of here immediately. We don't allow pets." I yelled back at her, "WHAT DO YOU MEAN YOU DON'T ALLOW PETS!!! YOU GROOMERS ARE ALL ALIKE! YOU WILL ONLY OWN UP TO YOUR GOOD WORK AND IGNORE US POOR WORKING STIFFS IF WE HAVE A PROBLEM!!"

Little did I know that the owner was right there in the shop listening to all this. He wouldn't even come over and admit who he was. I got more and more irate. "MY WIFE HAD OUR SHOW DOG GROOMED HERE LAST WEEK AND HIS HAIR IS FALLING OUT. LOOK HOW UPSET HE IS; HE KNOWS HE HAS A SHOW COM-

ING UP TOMORROW."

Freeway was running around in circles in a wild frenzy, just as he always does. Everyone in the shop was certain that I was an escapee from the local loony farm. The owner came to the desk to intervene. I threatened to sue him. I told him that I'd be driving that Rolls when my attorney got through with him. I told him I was taking "Farnsworth" (I thought that was a good name for an expensive show dog) to the car because he was so upset and that I would be back to deal with him.

Imagination can only tell what went on in that shop in the next two minutes! All the pressure that had built up was quickly released when I came back in singing *Happy Birthday*. The birthday boy couldn't stop laughing after he found out who sent me. I delivered his balloons and telegram and took Freeway home.

This twenty minute skit paid $100.00. Freeway still owes me, but I guess I'll have to cut him a break. He doesn't work all that often.

Tom Antion

Private Lessons

Let me tell you about Scanner, the Dalmatian my husband and I acquired last July as a sweet little six-week-old puppy. Her "yard" is the flat roof of our three-story home/electronics business building in Seattle, which is where she occasionally gets banished when she barks at customers.

As a young dog, Scanner was uncontrollable. I couldn't get her to do anything. I dutifully read all my "Train Your Dog in Seven Days" books from the library, but Scanner didn't seem to be getting past day one. We were even failing "Puppy school" class! This was not only embarrassing, it was very demoralizing for my competitive, perfectionist nature. Every week we would go to class, and every week she was the worst-behaving dog. Scanner was totally disobedient; wouldn't sit, stand, stay, or lay down; would bark, pee, and wag tail enthusiastically. Scanner was my first dog and things weren't going well.

Having your own business makes you determined, so we decided not to drop out of class. After four weeks my instructors felt sorry for me and offered remedial training. "It's time to establish who's the boss dog," said they. The next Sunday we met on the school parking lot for a SERIOUS lesson. The goal was to learn how to sit. My instructor took Scanner's leash, yanked the choke chain, pushed down her rear and said sternly, "SIT!" Scanner looked up at him, astonished, I had been asking her in my best reasonable voice to please *sit* down, if it weren't too much trouble. This man was giving an order and with no nonsense about it. When she didn't move fast enough to suit him the commands were firmly repeated. By the third round Scanner was on her haunches saying, "Yes, Sir and for how long, Sir?" I couldn't believe this was my dog!

Now it was my turn. With my instructor's help, my voice became firmer, my leash-yanking stronger, and my determination steelier. After wrestling Scanner to the ground a few times, slowly but surely I was becoming the boss dog to my dog. Perhaps my pup and I would make it after all.

Two hours later we walked with our heads held high! Scanner sat and lay down like a practically perfect lady. The next week in class I got an award for most improved.

Since then I couldn't say Scanner (or I) has been perfect, but I would say I am now a committed dog owner having great fun with my active, loving, reasonably obedient Dalmatian puppy! Come see her the next time you're in Seattle. She's sitting beside the front door, scanning the neighborhood.

Lynn Lively

The Dream

The blue and yellow flags that had been displayed with pride from the stands of the Pasadena Rose Bowl had all but disappeared. The green and yellow of Brazil were waving in unison from the boisterous sea of Brazilian supporters. Their team had just broken open a defensive struggle to produce a commanding lead in the semi-finals of the 1994 World Cup Soccer. The talented and precise Brazilians were now manhandling the surprising but overmatched Swedes. The powerful Swedish offense generated by Andersson, Brolin, and Ingesson seemed no match for the strong defense and pinpoint passing control of the Brazilians. The joy of the closing penalty kick heroics of the Swedish goalie Ravelli in their victory over Romania seemed a distant, and fast-fading memory.

But wait, a white and black flash with a blue and yellow collar raced past the outstretched arms of the referee and took to the field. As if possessed, the dog raced past defenders and leaped to head the ball past the shocked Brazilians. Using her snout and paws to stroke and control the ball, she shepherded the ball at break-neck speed toward the Brazilian goal. Surprise and laughter from the players and fans gave way to amazement as the dog centered the ball evading would be tacklers. As if rallying the fading spirits of the distressed Swedes, the blue and yellow flags were again raised to the heavens. Playing to the stands, the Dalmatian paused momentarily to raise her head in appreciative attention, and then darted and directed the ball across the field toward the goal. The fans were almost as enthusiastic as the referees were enraged by the talented but unwelcome distraction.

As millions watched around the world, the dog seemed to take control of her own private field of dreams. But the upstaged Brazilians had no intention of letting the dog have her way. A missed kick at the ball, only accelerated the precise antics of the dog. Racing first to the left and then the right, she moved gracefully past the attempted blocks and headed the ball past the outstretched arms of the Brazilian goalie. The announcer yelled for the world to hear, "Goooo...oooal!" The crowd went wild. The dog stopped to chew at the turf beneath her feet.

OK, so it didn't quite happen that way, but let's face it. Every dog has a dream. You know it's true; that's why their muscles twitch when you watch them dream in their dog beds.

An unlikely dream? Not if you know our dog, Sunshine. This three-year old Dalmatian has all the spunk, spirit and speed to give any soccer team a challenging run for their money. That's right! The dog plays soccer! With coiled feet ready to spring into action, she awaits your move. Dribble to the right, and she attacks. Kick the ball above her and she launches for a header. Either way, the ball is corralled and hurdled toward the goal.

So far, Sunshine hasn't made it to the World Cup. She's ready and we continue to practice. Teach an old dog new tricks? I say, you become an old dog when you stop doing tricks!

Dr. Terry Paulson

The
Babysitter

Everyone thinks that they have the best, the smartest, the prettiest, or most handsome dog. Mine was sure special to me.

We had received Bandit, a purebred Shihtzu, as a wedding present. I spoiled him as if he were my own baby. I worked with him to teach him words and he could pick out his toys by name and bring them to me.

I have a limp from an accident I was in as a teen-ager and have a number of other handicaps. Because I can't walk well, I wasn't sure how well I could take care of a human baby!

When I brought my baby daughter home from the hospital, Bandit was right there to help me take care of her. Anything that my daughter touched, Bandit loved to be around. He would sit in her baby seat, roll in her clothes, play with her toys.

When my daughter was very young, she had a hard time falling asleep. If I held her she would fall asleep easily, but because I jerked when I walked to put her in her crib, it would often wake her up if I had to get up to put her to bed. Because of this I would lay her on the couch next to me once she was asleep.

I'd lie there with her as long as I could, but those naps can be really long! My fear was that she would roll off the couch if I wasn't there protecting her. Bandit solved this problem for me.

His cue was: "Bandit, watch the baby." He would jump up on the couch and take my place next to my baby. If she would start to roll over in her sleep, he would gently roll her back against the back of the couch. Bandit and I both mothered the baby!

How this 10-pound "dumb" animal could come to my rescue time after time amazes me. Everyone

Hershkowitz

appreciates a good pet and I think the handicapped might appreciate them even more. I honestly believe that I would not have been as good a mother as I tried to be if it weren't for my Bandit.

Chris Hanse Baughman

The Boomerang Basset

My husband Garry and I staffed the phones for a small animal welfare group. The group takes in stray cats and dogs, fosters them in a home environment, and places them through advertisements and adoption days.

A recently acquired foster mom called us. A friend had rescued a basset hound and wanted to know if the group could foster it. Since the woman was willing and available to foster the dog, Garry told her we could accept it into the program. First, however, her friend would need to place a "found" notice in the paper.

When no one claimed the basset, he was delivered to his foster home. He received the usual physical exam, shots and neutering. Presently the dog was adopted. However, it didn't work out for the adopters. He barked too much and chewed things. In accordance with the group's policy, he was accepted back into the foster program and was placed in a new foster home.

Another ad was placed. Several people responded. The foster mom interviewed many candidates and chose a woman who already had a basset. When the foster mom dropped by to check on the progress of the dog, the adopter told her the dog ate too much food and she couldn't keep it. Besides, he barked too much.

Garry had kept a list of people who had responded too late to the advertisement. He called and told them the dog had been returned. If they were still interested in adopting a basset hound, he would arrange for them to visit the foster home.

A young woman adopted the dog. She just adored him. Three's a charm, we thought, as her adoption form was added to the basset's growing paper work. A few days later the woman called in tears. The dog barked all day which annoyed her neighbors, and he had destroyed her boyfriend's video tapes. She couldn't keep him.

Normally Garry and I only did administrative work. With all of the foster homes full, we told the woman to bring him by our house. Tears streamed down her face as she hugged him and kissed him good-bye for the last time. She begged us to find a good home for him. We assured her we would try, wondering if he would always come back like this.

We sympathized with those who had cared for him previously. He chewed up our sprinkler, and a food dish. When he wasn't destroying things, he howled a baleful basset wail. In fact, he wouldn't shut up!

To keep him quiet at night, Garry and I took to sleeping in separate quarters. I slept in the bedroom with our cat and dog (we were weary of our noisy guest), and my husband slept on the couch in the living room with a contented basset curled up on the floor.

A new advertisement was placed in the paper. When interested people called we were frank to the point of negativity. "He barks constantly and chews up everything," was our refrain. A few hardy souls made appointments.

One evening a nice couple with two young boys came by. It was love at first sight. We stressed to them his nasty habits. The lady said, "Oh, he's probably just lonely. I'm at home all day. It won't be a problem." They adopted the basset.

We cringed each time the phone rang. After a week passed we began to relax. The basset became a memory that had mellowed with time.

A few months later the phone rang. The couple was expecting another baby. The lady had developed complications which required that they give up their pet. Would we mind if they placed the animal on their own? Since they had had the dog for a while and were concerned about where he went, Garry acquiesced. In order to keep the records complete, he asked that they let him know when the dog was placed and with whom.

The man called to let us know the basset had been placed in a new home. He then told an amazing story. A woman responded to the ad. She and her husband had lost their basset hound several months

before. They were now ready to own another basset.   When she got the dog home, her husband
looked at it very closely. Their lost basset bore a
unique mark. This dog had the same mark. This
was their long lost dog!

Kathy Beth Macdonald

Proud Mama

Never having had a pet before, when I finally got my very own little miniature dachshund puppy, I was ecstatic!!! Me...a pet owner!

I took the training of this little four legged "person" VERY seriously, and everything seemed to be going fine except for one area. Whenever I took Toby out to "relieve" himself, I noticed that he would go to a certain spot and squat like a little girl dog. "Okay", I thought, "I guess I need to teach him how to lift his leg." Thus began an intense "training regime" of leg lifting.

Every time I took Toby out, I would take him over

to a tree, scoot him close to it, and lift his little back leg. Each time I did this, Toby would turn his head and just stare at me with a look that said, "just WHAT do you think you are doing?!?!?!?" ... He would yank his foot away, and then go over to his "spot" and squat! Frustration!!!!!

But, I didn't give up...this routine became a daily ritual. I never wavered in my determination...my little boy dog was going to learn to lift his leg! Finally, one day in the middle of a walk, Toby went to a bush and LIFTED HIS LEG!!! all by himself. I was thrilled...so thrilled that I couldn't help but brag a little.

My bragging came to a sudden halt when I heard the gales of laughter. As I listened to the words between the gasps for air, it suddenly dawned on me that Toby would have learned this little "number" on his own. And, the only thing I really accomplished was making a complete fool of myself!!! You see, throughout the entire "training" I had been observed by several VERY amused neighbors...and many who did not even know my name dubbed me as "the lady who lifts her dog's leg!"

Gail Wenos, CSP, CPAE

Hard Lessons

I would like to share a story about my dog. His name is Star Spaniel Banner We just call him Banner. He is a 13-year-old English Cocker Spaniel. He and I have been together through my marriage and divorce and the 8 years of my son's life. In fact, my son and I argue about whose dog he really is (mine or his).

A few year's ago when I lived in Austin, Texas, we lived out in the country across the street from a greenbelt. While my family and I were gone for the day, Banner decided that he had quite enough of being alone in the backyard and dug a hole under the fence. He must have heard noise coming from the greenbelt and thought he would sow some wild oats with whatever animal he could find! Unfortunately, the animals turned out to be some wild boys who were shooting bows and arrows and they shot my lovely little Banner.

My neighbors found him on the side of the road and called us. Well, as you can imagine, I fell apart thinking that I was about to lose by best friend. I rushed home and put him in my car to transport him to the emergency clinic. He had lost a lot of blood and his breathing was very shallow. I had to keep patting his head to keep him awake — I was so afraid he was going to die any minute and I just wasn't ready to accept that. He was, however, licking my hand the entire time because I was bawling so hard that he was upset.

He was thinking about me the whole time — what a dog! They did exploratory surgery and would you believe that the arrow did not hit any vital organs. He did lose a lot of blood but they were able to supply him with enough to bring him around. It took about a week for him to get back to normal again. He hasn't dug any holes under the fence lately.

Now, if he can just pass that lesson on to our new 7-month old Newfoundland puppy!

Dana Murphy

Royal K-9

Once in a lifetime, or so it seems, a special pet is sent by the Almighty to watch over his/her master although the lines between who is master often blur. Most often this pet is a dog. A cat won't fetch a slipper without eating it, a horse is hard to housebreak, and snakes are often indifferent to commands. But a dog can be a member of the family. Such is the case with Princess.

The runt of the litter, nobody wanted Princess. We gave away ten brothers and sisters within 24 hours of the ad in the paper, but the little runt that everybody passed over stayed behind. We decided to keep her a couple of extra weeks, put her on a power diet, exercise program, and maybe she would grow to be the size of our veterinary bill. And, it worked!

Some man came to look at her and actually said they'd take her but it didn't feel like his heart was sincere. My wife suddenly changed her mind. She wanted to keep Princess. She had potential and would make a sweet, cuddly lap dog, she decided. That was two years and 40 pounds ago. People always want to know her breed. I tell them she is a short-haired, miniature, Somali-Collie/Water Spaniel/Airedale.

Isn't it funny how things are not always what they seem?

Doc Blakely

Dinner Time

We have an English Bulldog. I wanted something at my home that looked worse than I did when I came home from a two-week speaking tour! She fits the bill perfectly. Beaulah is part of our family, she eats and sleeps and snores like a Bull when she does both. She is part pig and all love!

Beaulah was six years old and we had her bred to a beautiful white male. Our son Carter, we call him "Little Bubba," was six also and very excited about the whole affair. Everyday he would ask, "How much longer?", "When?", "Is she OK?" and "When does the puppy come?" Bulldogs often have a single pup, and three is unusual. He had named it already!

We were almost sorry we had decided to breed the dog, he was driving us nuts!!

Little Bubba waited on Beaulah hand and foot, watched her grow and even kept a journal of the blessed event!

The "DAY" came and of course she gave birth under the house while Little Bubba was at school. I crawled under, got them and put her and one brown and white wrinkled faced female and one pure white male in a box in the garage. She was worn out and most appreciative of my efforts!

When my son came home that day, he ran from the school bus yelling, "It came today, didn't it?" I was amazed at his certainty, but small children and puppies have ESP we adults do not understand. I assured him that they had and there were two of them! He yelled out, "Wow, where are they?"

I took him to the garage and the puppies, not 10 hours old, were nestled up against Beulah's fat belly nursing for the first time. They were sucking and grunting with their faces completely out of sight! Little Bubba looked at this sight and was completely dumbfounded. For a moment he watched in pure wonder and then looked up at me with the most puzzled look on his face I had ever seen and asked, "What are they doing?" I replied like a proud father in my most matter of fact voice, "They are eating!" He looked back down at the marvelous sight, watched for a minute, then looked up with an even more worried look and asked, "Skin?"

Bubba Bechtol

Tennis Anyone?

I have a beautiful light-colored golden retriever named Joshua; we call him Josh.

One day, I was watching a tennis match on TV. Josh, who loves to play with tennis balls, was watching with me. His head moved back and forth and back and forth as he followed the ball going from one side of the screen to the other.

Suddenly the ball went out of camera range and disappeared. Josh got up, went behind the TV set, and searched for the missing tennis ball.

Allen Klein, CSP

Only a Dog

Divi was by far the best dog we've ever had. His scrawny body, beagle-like ears and thin haunches were ours for almost ten years.

He arrived, unexpectedly, on a Sunday afternoon. My husband, intending only to pick up our son at a birthday party, stopped at a pet shop on the way and came home with a $10 dog. We had discussed the possibility of a puppy and I had always said no! I knew who the caretaker would be, and I was not looking for more responsibility at the time.

In with the co-conspirators, came this wild fur ball! The puppy barked at my guests and within minutes had terrorized our two children. He was actually gnawing on one of the kids! All eyes were on me. What would I do? Should I just yell, "Take him back!" I really like animals, I just didn't see the need for one.

"Uh oh, there's going to be a divorce!" said one of my friends. And so, Divi, short for Divorce, was named. Divi never did anything extraordinary - and he certainly didn't live up to his name! He gave us love unconditionally and often reminded us how to do the same.

He'd slip out of the backyard gate, take off for a few hours and show up at the back door, pawing at the glass to be let in, trying to fool us into thinking he had never left.

He'd protect us by barking loudly when the door-bell rang (more out of fear than ferociousness) but would welcome the visitors in once they were cleared by the family.

He wouldn't give up his search for his favorite toy, an orange rubber whale, left over from the boys' bath toys, when I'd ask him to find it. Sometimes I'd have to help him find it because he would just keep searching!

Only once was Divi groomed by a professional. He came back looking exactly the same as when he left! He had the sweetest personality. I could take his food from his mouth without so much as a dirty look from his eyes. He was so gentle. The boys would pull on him and poke him, and his only move would be to (wisely) hide under the bed.

As the boys grew older, so did Divi. He was a valued member of our family and we gave him the best care possible when he developed heart disease. He died in my arms one morning when the boys were at school and my husband, Paul, was in a meeting with a customer. I cried as I held Divi and when it was over, I called Paul to let him know. As we cried with each other over the phone, I heard the customer impatiently say, "Oh, it's only a dog."

Only a dog? Not our Divi.

Nancy Hershkowitz

Special Delivery

I live in a quiet neighborhood in San Clemente away from all the hustle and bustle of major California cities. Gizmo and I are very happy there. Gizmo is a 14 year old Shitzu, weighing in at a robust 9 pounds.

One day last November, I took Gizmo out for her usual morning walk. Each work day we walk, Gizmo and I have breakfast and then we "commute" to another room - my home office. Basically, this is our routine day in and day out. This particular day, Gizmo, upon approaching home, planted herself at the end of the driveway refusing to budge. I called for her, "Gizmo, come on. Come on, Sweetie!" It was no use. She wasn't moving. It's a quiet street, and she seemed safe, wasn't in the street, so I shrugged my shoulders and went inside.

From my office window, as the day passed, I could see my little fur ball at the end of the driveway. She hadn't moved but a few inches all day! As it was starting to get dark, I called for her again, this time refusing to take no for an answer. Reluctantly, Gizmo did come in, ate her dinner and eventually went to bed.

The next morning, we set out for the usual routine and sure enough Gizmo again stopped at the end of the driveway. "What are you doing??" I asked puzzled, somehow hoping to get an answer. All I got were her big coal eyes staring up at me as if to say. "Gee Mom, I'm a big girl, I'll be all right!" (Actually, she would be about 98 in people years!) I went inside, leaving her as she requested.

About 11:00 AM, I glanced up from my desk to see Gizmo, on all fours, attentively peering down the street, her tail wagging passionately. Making its way down the street, was the familiar red, white and blue truck of the postal service. As I got to the door, I saw Gizmo heading to the stopped truck. The mailman knelt down, and handed Gizmo a bone! "I hope you don't mind" said the mailman seeing me, "I give your little dog a cookie every morning."

"Oh, that explains it!" as the proverbial light bulb in my head went off. "She waited for you all day yesterday."

"Oh, I'm sorry! Yesterday was Veteran's Day, and I had the day off."

Jodi Rudick

Takin' Care
of Grandma

We used to have an old dog that just came to our place. Her teeth were worn and she was already gray about the mouth, so we called her "Grandma." She was one of those characters that everyone loved and inquired about. Strangers or folks who didn't know about her used to cut their eyes from side to side when they heard the following conversation.

"How's Grandma. She still alive?"

"Yeah, but her teeth are worn so bad that about all we let her have is chopped liver and corn bread."

"I'll bet if you gave her a raw egg and wormed her, the old gal would perk up. That's a good remedy for anybody's Grandma."

"We tried that once but she ran up under the house and we had to turn the hose on her to get her out. When Pat grabbed her by the leg she nearly gummed his thumb off. She scaled that picket fence around the house and spent the rest of the day limping like she was hurt, looking for sympathy."

One day this do-gooder who just couldn't stand it any longer suggested that the elderly should get more respect even if we were just kidding about our Grandma. To which we would reply. "We ain't kidding'. We love Grandma. That's the main reason we came to town today, to let her ride in the truck. She always liked to hang her head out the door and slobber in the wind."

"Grandma used to hide in the grass by the side of the road for hours and when an old, slow, rattletrap would come chugging by, she would attack. For about ten years she would make that driver think a crazed Banshee was about to deliver him from among the living. The rest of the day she would just lay up next to the water trough and grin."

To top off our day the Widow Perkins passed by and sweetly said, "Hello, boys. How's Grandma? Do bring her over for a visit. I just love the way she lays on her back and lets me scratch her belly."

That's when the do-gooders start looking behind them and backing out the door.

Lots of people are just waiting in the wings to jump to conclusions without the burden of facts. Never believe anything you hear and only half of what you see.

Doc Blakely

Cute as a Button

It was our daughter's tenth birthday and my husband and I agreed a cocker spaniel would be the perfect surprise. Instead it was a tail wagging mutt - a tan curly haired terrier with long cocker spaniel ears and red eyelashes - who captured our hearts as we walked through the animal shelter. She was as "cute as a button" and Buttons joined the family.

Before Grandma and Grandpa came to live with us, the three children and Bob and I, would pile into the car each Saturday and drive 30 miles to visit them. Buttons loved car trips! She would be the first one out of the house and she would leap into the car and climb into her spot, the back window ledge of the car! There she would sleep until we'd turn off the parkway onto Grandma and Grandpa's street. As soon as we'd make that turn, Buttons would wake up and start sniffing. Somehow she knew which turn was the turn that meant her special treat wasn't far away.

Buttons loved Grandma and Grandpa and when they moved in with us, Buttons and Grandpa were inseparable. We weren't sure who enjoyed those daily walks more! As Grandpa became weaker, however, his shaky legs made him reluctant to take her on the leash. The first time he left the house without her, Buttons jumped on his bed and pulled holes in his bed cover. It was the only act of rebellion we ever witnessed in sixteen years and we wondered if it was sadness or frustration that made her do it.

Buttons kept herself busy patrolling her territory. Bootsy, the neighbor cat, would often stray into our yard. Buttons, realizing the enemy was in her sites, would quickly chase Bootsy off the property. As soon as Bootsy reached her own driveway she would stop dead in her tracks and glare at Buttons. Buttons knew better than to follow her into "enemy territory." She would back off and yelp as if she had been struck. We soon realized only her ego had been hurt - Bootsy was rightfully on her own property and was daring Buttons to come forward.

Buttons was our faithful companion for sixteen years. Our children grew up and left for college and marriage. The day our first grandchild was born, more than twenty years ago, Buttons left our world. As smart as she was, we think she knew the new grandbaby was "cute as a button" and this would be the perfect time for her to make her exit.

Ida Morrison

Sweet Partings

My perfect, most gorgeous, queen of the countryside, always smiling, saved from the pound 9 years ago, golden retriever named Casey Indiana Jones, the love of my dog life, had never done much wrong in her life UNTIL just last month. I was leaving for Europe on business and two nights before a very early morning departure, I took my passport in its fine Italian leather case and placed it on my desk. Not thinking much about it, I went out to dinner. Upon returning home, I found Casey hiding in the bathroom and my passport case and its contents shredded on the dining room floor.

Luckily, the US Passport office was open the next

morning and I was able to secure an emergency replacement passport in just a few hours.

I surmised that doggie instincts might be much better than my own and wondered if intercontinental travel was indeed wise. But logic prevailed and I reckoned that Miss Jones, who was reared on rawhide, found the aroma of fine leather too good to pass up. The passport was really incidental.

But my showing up at the passport office with a mutilated document in a zip lock bag "Sorry officer, the dog ate my homework" must have been a sight to be seen.

Karma? The trip to Europe was a huge success. Downside? I lost 4 years worth of really cool visas and entry stamps - memories - gone but not forgotten.

It made me feel kind of good to know Casey would try every trick in the book to keep me at home!

David Kliman

Instinct

H er name was Heather. She was a Shetland Sheep dog, A.K.A. Sheltie, that we had for thirteen years before she died of old age.

Sheltie herding ability is legendary. That's their purpose in life. It's instinctive.

Years ago, I marveled as I watched Heather crisscross only inches in front of my six year old son David's bike as he rode around the neighborhood. It amazed me how Heather could match her speed to David's. If David was speeding down a hill, Heather was speeding barely in front of him, herding him on his bicycle. If David was enjoying a leisurely bike ride, there Heather was again — only inches from David's front wheels, matching her speed to his.

One day, my husband Ken, my one year old daughter Dana, and I were in the driveway near the front yard, playing catch with Heather. Ken wandered to the back of the house looking for David. I heard the phone ring and went inside to answer it thinking Ken was still watching the baby.

I heard Heather barking excitedly from the front lawn. I looked out the window and what I saw terrified me. A car was coming down the hill on the street in front of our house. Dana, the baby, was toddling toward the street.

Heather was frantically barking and "herding" her. When that didn't stop Dana from her intended goal, the street, Heather knocked her to the ground. The baby got up, somewhat unsteadily, and once again tottered toward the street. Again, Heather herded her and knocked her to the ground, all the while barking wildly and looking toward the house.

Instinctually she knew that Dana was in imminent

danger, herded her to safety and alerted those of us with less well developed instincts!

Patricia Ball, CSP, CPAE

Special Privileges

My wife made it very clear to our dog that there are inside toys and there are outside toys. When the dog tried to bring a stick into the house my wife stopped her with a sharp, "No, no! Sticks are for the outside."

Two weeks ago the dog gave me a "Boy you're gonna be in big trouble" look when in through the front door I dragged our Christmas tree.

Ron Dentinger

Memories

The lucky ones lived in the past. Some were confined with restraints for their own safety. Others shuffled around aimlessly, resigned to spending the rest of their days in an indigent-care nursing home. Some were visited by family members on weekends and holidays. A few were all alone, having outlived their children, or been abandoned by them. They all longed for a loving touch.

Two year old Heather had love to spare. My husband and I adopted her from the local Humane Society when she was eight months young. A Terrier-Spitz with a Pomeranian face, she delights in meeting people. She hops on legs made of springs, stretches out her arms, and gives little kisses to anyone who will accept them. I felt a trip to the nursing home was in order.

Heather was on her best behavior. Black lips in a perpetual grin, she made the rounds and greeted everyone. Hands, which spent most days folded in laps, stretched out to touch her. Faces lit with joy when she wiggled in greeting. Men chuckled and women laughed at her loving kisses.

When they saw her, she reminded them of happy times. They told stories about dogs who had accompanied them on their farm rounds and about pampered animal friends who learned to sit daintily on chairs covered with lace doilies.

One woman's reaction will forever be etched in my mind. She hugged my little dog to her, and began to cry. After awhile, I gently lifted Heather from the woman's grasp. I held the woman until there were no more tears. For a moment, we had all been touched by love.

Kathy Beth Mcdonald

Elvis

I always wanted a dog named Elvis. So nine years ago when I got my English Bulldog, I named her Elvis. I know you're wondering if she reminded me of Elvis. Not so much, when I got her, however, I have noticed now how much she has become like her famous namesake. All she has done since I got her is get fatter and fatter and she spends most of her time watching TV. Funny, how when you give your dog a name, they become like the name. My other dog, Nixon, for instance. He's a German Shepherd and not long ago ate my audio cassette tape. It wasn't that bad, though because we only lost 17 1/2 minutes of it.

Although many people would say Elvis is ugly, to me, she is beautiful. She is the one thing that I can always count on to be happy to see me and to make me smile. Her smashed in face and bulging eyes and teeth that stick out never fail to make me want to reach down and scratch her fat little tummy.

A great deal of my success in the speaking business is due to Elvis. I am known as the speaker with all the weird glasses. Kind of like Elton John, but better! I have over 25 pairs of glasses in various shapes and colors. And it's all because of Elvis.

When I first started in the business, I wore boring brown glasses like everyone else. Then one morning I got up and reached for my glasses in the place where I always leave them. To my surprise they weren't there. I had to find those glasses. I walked into our living room and there in my chair (a place where she was definitely not supposed to be) was Elvis and a half-eaten pair of brown glasses. She looked at me with so much guilt in her eyes and she looked so pitiful because she knew that she had messed up bad , that I couldn't even get mad. I took what was left - the lens - and off I went with my blurry vision to replace the glasses. When I got there, the only frames that would fit the lens and that could be done quickly were bright blue. Oh well, I needed them so I took them.

The next speech I gave was done in bright blue glasses. A few days later I received a call from a man who attended that speech. The guy wasn't sure that he had the right speaker so he said, "Are you the one with the blue glasses?" I confessed that I was. He said, "I wasn't sure of your name, but I'll never forget those glasses." I decided right then to use glasses to make myself even more memorable. I immediately bought red glasses; then green; then polka-dot. The list goes on and on. And I keep getting calls for the guy with the glasses. My income and my career have flourished - all because of a fat ugly dog named Elvis.

You know you never can tell when near disaster brings great opportunity!

Larry Winget

The Fisherdog

Tosha, our little Sheltie mix, previously a quiet withdrawn puppy, has turned into an obsessive, compulsive fisher-dog! Quite by chance one evening, looking for a way to entertain her, I took a fishing rod, put a tiny bug size piece of cloth on the line and then cast the line eight feet into the living room. When Tosha saw the "fish" wiggle on the line, she froze. And as soon as I jerked on the line she dove for her prize!

Picture this. Comfortable in my recliner, I now entertain my dog by swinging a fishing rod back and forth in my living room! Attached to the eight foot line is a tiny piece of cloth and attached to that is a twenty pound blur trying to catch it! Occasionally, I give in and let the " fish" land. Tosha stops dead in her tracks and stalks it - carefully - waiting for it to move again.

Sometimes, though not often, she'll catch it. She calmly takes it over to her favorite spot to just savor it for a while! She holds it still until after a bit, she'll get up, drop it and start stalking it again. That's her indication to me that I have to uphold my end of this expedition and make the "fish" move for her. If I don't do it quickly enough, she looks at me pathetically. If I still don't do it, she barks.

Tosha and I fish for about three hours each evening. Starting time is after work - about 6:30pm. I don't know how she tells the time, but I know she does because if I don't start casting by 6:30, she politely rests her little head on my leg - and doesn't budge until I can't resist any longer! (Resting her head quietly and begging is a lot better than when she used to drag the fishing rod to me - in my home office!)

And if we dare to go out for the evening, do you think she would greet us like a puppy, happy to see us home? Not Tosha!! As soon as she hears us returning, she positions herself on the back of the couch right under the fishing rod and keeps jumping, desperately trying to grasp the tip of the rod! Guess it's never too late for a fisher-dog!!

Calvin Coolidge was right when he said, "Nothing in the world can take the place of persistence!" Or of Tosha!

Jim Weems

The
Business Trip

When Dottie, my Afghan Hound, was six months old, a friend from Atlanta called to say he would be passing through Phoenix on his way to San Diego and wondered if he could stay with me for a few weeks. I told him it would be a pleasure to have him as a guest. Unfortunately, I had a business trip planned for the first three days of his visit but we coordinated a way for him to get my house key. His visit was a welcome one, not only because I had not seen him for a long time but also because Dottie could remain at home with him instead of going to the kennel. I cautioned him that Dottie was mischievous and he assured me that Dottie was in good hands - he had years of experience with dogs.

When I returned from my trip, my friend picked me up at the airport. How had he and Dottie gotten along, I asked. He just laughed. It seems that the first day he arrived Dottie was somewhat leery of him and kept her distance.

The next morning she woke him at 5:00 AM wanting to go outside. He opened the arcadia door and let her into the back yard. As he wanted to get at least a few more hours sleep, he left the door open about two feet so she could come and go at her leisure. He awoke around 8:30 AM and remembered thinking how quiet the house was. He also remembered thinking how good Dottie had behaved since his arrival and that my initial cautions about her behavior were unfounded. As he walked toward the arcadia door looking out into the backyard, he saw Dottie sitting regally in the middle of the yard surrounded by the entire contents of his suitcase - socks, underwear, swim trunks (which no longer contained a crotch!), shirts, pants, shorts, shoes, toiletries - everything was there.

I apologized profusely for my child's behavior but couldn't help laughing. He assured me that he could have more easily recovered from Dottie's unpacking escapade had it not been for the automatic sprinklers that came on just as he began to pick up his clothes!

Ruth Guzley

Doggie Tails

My older sister's wedding was planned to be an "intimate" gathering. Three hundred of our family and friends were invited to the downtown Chicago hotel to join in the celebration.

Oliver, our eight pound black poodle, wasn't originally on the guest list. Tammie, my younger sister, and I thought this was clearly an oversight. After all, Oliver was a member of our family and should not only be an invited guest - he should be a member of the bridal party!

This idea actually appealed to our dad, but it was immediately vetoed by Mom. This didn't stop Tammie and me.

Armed with white and black material, rhinestone buttons and silver sequins, we visited a family friend. What we needed was a tuxedo, with tails, for Oliver.

On Linda's wedding day, I carried Oliver in my garment bag and sequestered him in my hotel room. Initially he seemed kind of confined, but after an order from room service, he was quite content

I waited until after the ceremony, retrieved Oliver and let him wander among the guests in the reception area. He looked resplendent in his formal wear.

Mom was fuming at first, but eventually she appreciated both the joke and his presence. Somewhere between the reception's conclusion and the dinner's commencement, however, mom lost track of Oliver! She was frantic as she scurried through the hotel's lobby asking, "Excuse me, but have you seen a black poodle in a white tuxedo?"

Tammi and I could have told mom that we knew exactly where Oliver was. He was where he always is during dinner - sitting at our feet beneath the head table!

Jeff Blackman

Angels

The dogs, Dudley and Buckwheat, were born in the summer about 15 years ago. They had a big problem though - they had no Mama.

My daughter, Andi, was working at a center dedicated to helping stray and unwanted dogs find a home.

Of course, almost every dog that came in, of every size, Andi wanted to bring home with her. I remember Mindy, a Yorkshire Terrier, who we kept until she went on to the great dog playground in the sky. And then there was a large German police dog who we fortunately placed with some close friends.

Dudley and Buckwheat had no Mama to sustain them in their early days and they were to be put to sleep immediately. Andi let us know that we had to give these two helpless little guys a chance. The thought of them growing up to become gigantic Doberman hounds in our home, had to be accepted.

Andi, her sister, Vicki, and my wife, Ginger fed the pups with milk at regular intervals all day and night. When the pups began to move around a bit, Ginger insisted that one Doberman was all we could possibly hope to handle.

With meticulous care, Andi put Buckwheat up for adoption. A fine young boy who lived on a farm in Indiana fell in love with our little brown Buckwheat.

Dudley turned out not to be a Doberman after all. I'm not sure, but I believe a mix between a cocker spaniel and a dachshund is pretty accurate.

Never in the history of dogdom has there been a more dedicated watch dog. With his ferocious bark, he kept the mailman at bay every delivery day ...

and the trashman alert during his visit each week!

When Andi took Dudley to obedience school, he outshined every thoroughbred by a country mile. Those elite dogs couldn't hold a candle to the quick learning intellect Dudley.

Oh, and he's not just intelligent - he smiles a lot too. You look at his face and you can see plain as day that he is smiling broadly when something strikes him funny.

As you realize I'm sure, I could go on and on. Dudley truly made us realize one thing: God wanted to bring angels to the earth and teach us about unconditional love. That's why he invented dogs.

Arnold Nick Carter

Fraternity Brothers

Chesty was the Sigma Chi Fraternity mascot at Arizona State University. He was a sheppard-mix mutt. Reports vary on when this over protective beast made his way onto the ASU campus...1981 or 1982, maybe. He was rescued and trained by à marine who instilled those Marine values into his brainy dog.

Chesty was so well known on campus that any Sigma Chi who spotted him roaming around could actually take him into class without any objection from professors. His attendance record was probably better than most guys in the house! He made his way onto campus by waiting for green lights before he would cross the street, the busiest street in town.

He was loyal. Our chapter had 100-plus members in it with 30 or 40 changes every year. Chesty never barked at the brothers and, because of chivalry, never at women. He was very protective of each one of us. He even bit an ASU police officer who was breaking up a fight between one of our less-active brothers and another guy. He thought the officer was involved in the skirmish and came to the Sigma Chi's defense.

He was a warrior. One summer, 1986, our neighboring fraternity was supposed to take care of him. They didn't. Chesty suffered through an Arizona summer scavenging for food and water to survive. When we returned his ever-present wagging tail and thin body anxiously greeted us.

He was neat. He was taught to never walk on the dining room floor or in the kitchen. Twice in my three years there did I see him cross the dining room floor (I never ever saw him in the kitchen.) Both times were emergencies—like a ruckus out on Alpha Drive that he had to go bark at.

He was also a bit of a party animal. During parties any glass of beer set on the gound would be tipped over and the contents lapped up. Chesty wasn't brand conscious but did like his beer cold. The following day was an all-too-familiar sight. Fran, the house mother, was grinding an aspirin into Chesty's food while he lay quietly (hung over?!?) on the front lawn.

These are just a few tales of the most infamous dog to walk the ground at ASU. He was actually pictured in the ASU yearbook...while our fraternity picture didn't make it in. He "graduated" in 1988, I believe in Humanities, and went to live a relaxing life at my dad's until he passed away in May, 1995.

Rick Kiburz

Alpha Dog

"ELLIE! ELLIE-E-E-, N-O-O-O-O...!" My horrified screams sharply pierced the peaceful, rural fall afternoon. The entire neighborhood surely jumped at the sudden sound of my alarm. Elllie, our newly adopted 110 lb. Alaskan malamute, appeared oblivious. The pride I had felt in bringing her home to my new husband two days earlier was swiftly evaporating into dismay.

She was at this moment hurtling with deadly silence at breakneck speed down the road toward a small black cocker spaniel a couple of hundred feet away. The unrestrained spaniel, out for a leisurely walk

with a mother and two children, showed a total ar-
ray of emotions within a few seconds. She went from
a happy friendliness, to uncertain hesitation and finally to sheer terror, recognizing the victim she was.
Ellie struck.

That was to be the first of many assaults that I was
to break up between Elllie and her victims. The
posture was to become familiar: Ellie on top, the
other dog underneath. I would break up the fight
using my feet, hands and a violent shriek. Amazingly, as was true of every subsequent battle that
involved any kind of human intervention, she
seemed to be very aware of what was dog and what
was not. I was never left with so much as a scratch.

Meanwhile, I dragged my lunging she-monster back
to our nearby house, and raced out to the terrorized family (and thankfully, unhurt dog) with pro-
fuse apologies. They were blessedly forgiving once
they had calmed down, and took their quivering,
traumatized dog home - wet between the legs and
dignity badly mauled.

Fortunately, this was the extent of the damage in-
flicted on Ellie's chosen victims. She seemed to need
only to injure any possible feelings of superiority to

accomplish her purpose, and she really seemed to enjoy her work. Had I understood at that time the term "alpha" with regard to canines - that some dogs are simply born to dominate - I might've been less chagrined about Ellie's confrontations. The fact that all dogs are descendants of wolves and therefore retain wolf behavior to some extent was not an area I had yet explored. Later I would understand that Ellie, as a malamute, was more wolf-like than most domestic dogs - in appearance as well as behavior - and most surely would have been the undisputed leader of any pack in the wild. But, at that time, I found the prospect of being her primary guardian a formidable assignment.

If this were what Ellie was all about, the story would end here. I could not have put up with this level of stressful emotion for long. But from the beginning, Ellie revealed intriguing complexities of the Jekyl/Hyde nature and what you aroused in her depended on whether you had two legs or four. If you were human - any human - you were greeted by an extraordinary gentle and loving nature. Her striking beauty and exquisite features were accompanied by a curiously demure, unassuming and accepting personality that seemed to touch the softness in everyone she met. She was a dog that turned heads on streets, that people wanted to touch, to comment on, to just stand back and admire. She would quietly and graciously accept all gestures of affection with noble dignity and open fondness, almost always genteely offering her signature forepaw the way a lady offers her hand.

Her manner with children was especially tender. No matter how small, children were rarely intimidated, and would run up to her with delight. She was exceedingly patient with overly eager displays of affection and would move slowly and carefully, seemingly aware that her hugeness could inflict injury or fright. I was to particularly value this gift later when our daughter, Kayla, joined the family. Even after Kayla became capable of unintentionally aggressive advances, I never had to worry that Ellie would lose her patience. She never did.

But what truly made me stop short of absolute exasperation with Ellie's "alpha genes" was what I began to see as her true essence, something that felt almost otherworldly. At times, looking into her slanted dark eyes, enhanced by the natural black eyeliner and a pure white face, I had the sense that she was thousands of years old. Her unconditional love, tolerance and acceptance of all people in addition to an uncanny emotional maturity seemed to have evolved from an ancient, highly spiritual wisdom. Initially, I felt a bit sheepish and somewhat private about this intimate perception, but the sense only grew over time.

Not knowing her age when we adopted her, our best guess was that she was about ten. That seemed young to me for her to be aging so notably, but I did know that for a big dog she was considered "geriatric." I began watching her closely.

The late April evening when she couldn't make it up the hill to home, I knew Ellie was facing more than benign aging. With a cold sense of dread, I made a veterinary appointment. Two mornings later we were at the vet who could find nothing immediately apparent. She took a blood test and suggested Ellie may have hurt her back. I leaped on that possibility like a dog being thrown a juicy bone. Oh yes, I thought with sudden cheeriness. Nothing a little aspirin wouldn't help.

The next day the vet called back. "I think it would be a good idea to bring her in tomorrow for x-rays," she said. I told her I noticed Ellie seemed to be breathing heavier, then hastily added, "But you know, it's a warm day and she's laying in the sun.

My now almost three year old daughter and I dropped Ellie off the next morning. I called back several hours later for a report and learned the vet had scheduled an ultrasound appointment for later that afternoon with an internal specialist. The x-rays showed a cloudiness with what appeared to be fluid in her chest and abdomen. Her words, "I don't think you should wait" drew me into a swirling orbit of unreality.

The following three hours were the last I was to spend with Ellie. As I sat at the specialist's clinic with Ellie's head in my arms, I watched together with the vet as an ultrasound probe revealed a heart based tumor, now so large it was consuming her breathing space. All my optimistic hopes for a treatable discovery were slowly dissolving at the sight of the cold, harsh image of a malignant mass. I laid my head on hers, fingers clinching her fur, and stared at her shaven chest now rising and falling laborious. How could such corrupt tissue grow in such a gracious being? Ellie, her character true to the end, had quietly tolerated all the discomfort, inconvenience and difficulties of this exceedingly long day with her usual patience and forgiveness.

With a heart full of grief but the knowledge that nothing could be done to heal her body, I knew it was time to release her from what had become an uncomfortable place to be.

She was given a lethal dose in the back of our van by our local vet. I knelt beside her, quietly sobbing. Ellie, impervious to pain, did not react to the entry of the needle and patiently waited, looking at nothing in particular. Then, she suddenly raised her eyes, first looking into mine and then straight at the vet. There was an unmistakable sense that she knew. Ellie knew what was happening. I was sure of it.

Within ten seconds she closed her eyes, her huge tail became relaxed and the life force left her. Ellie was gone, leaving her massive, beautiful body with us in the van. I drove us home.

My husband and I buried Ellie very early the next morning on our property under the tree that had become her favorite place to lay in the past few months.

Tim and I routinely tell "Ellie stories." The more we have contemplated, the more we agree that somehow it was really Ellie's choice to leave, that her illness didn't so much destroy her as it was a vehicle for her ultimate freedom.

I like to fancy that her years with us was her earthly purpose this time around, and that her leaving when she did meant her work was complete. Perhaps she'll return someday to live out an existence with another student in need of valuable lessons. And maybe next time she'll even like dogs.

Sherrie K. Evenson

Thank you!

A percentage of all profits from Dog Tales of the Heart will be donated to The Seeing Eye, Inc. (a non-profit organization whose primary purpose is to help people who are blind achieve independence and mobility through the use of properly trained dog guides) or Canine Companions, Inc. (a non-profit organization dedicated to making everyday tasks easier for people with disabilities other than blindness).

Who is

Sue A. Hershkowitz?

S ue Hershkowitz has spoken before more than three-quarters of a million people both nationally and internationally during the past 14 years. She holds degrees in English and Counseling and earned a fellowship sponsored by the University of California at Berkeley.

Her client list reads like a Who's Who of major corporations and associations including Marriott Hotels and Resorts, IBM, Walt Disney Studios, Prudential Realty, Motorola and American Express.

Sue is a member of the Board of Directors of the National Speakers Association and has earned her Certified Speaking Professional designation. This designation has been earned by fewer than 300 NSA members and recognizes Sue's commitment, integrity and experience in the field of professional speaking. In addition, she has served on the editorial advisory board of Meeting Professionals International and the industry advisory board for MeetingNews.

Sue's keynotes and training workshops will change the way you do business. Whether it's a keynote focusing on *The Future is for the Open Minded* , a general session on *Hyperservice*™, a Sales training session on *Power Writing*™, or a workshop on *You Think I Said What?*, you'll laugh while you learn practical, cutting edge skills to enhance productivity, professionalism and profits.

Sue loves what she does and her energy and enthusiasm are contagious. Her presentations inspire, motivate and educate.

To contact Sue for further information,
or to schedule her for a presentation,
please write to:

High Impact Presentations
14826 North 54th Pl.
Scottsdale, AZ 85254

Call 1-602-996-8864
or
e-mail Sue at
AOL at *Hershk*
or
Compuserve at 74117,56.

Contributors

Patsy Hall is in the entertainment production and Speaker Bureau business with her husband, Dick, in St. Louis. Their Labrador, Joe Hall, is also part of the regular office staff. Dick used to be a poodle breeder — Patsy has had up to fourteen bird dogs at a time. Joe, presently an only child, lives with two cats and a bird.

Bryan Townsend is a professional speaker and author of the book <u>Life Is An adventure</u>. He lives in Talladega, Alabama.

Suzanne Vaughn. As a professional speaker, Suzanne presents Keynotes, Personal Management Seminars & Youth Programs enhanced with "Real Life" Humor, Stories & Inspiration. 1-303-690-2300.

Joy Fox, International Meeting Planner, also trainer — protocol and etiquette for children and adults (905)825-8061. Dog and cat lover — will never be without a 4 legged friend - they're wonderful!

Joachim de Posada is an international speaker, trainer, consultant on management, motivational sales and marketing. Call 305-471-9887.

Twyman L. Towery, Ph.D., FACHE, is a professional speaker, management consultant and author. In Twyman's latest book, *The Wisdom of Wolves: Nature's Way to Organizational Success*, he responds to the resurgence of respect for the natural world with a guide to assist today's businessperson in meeting one of the greatest challenges: to find a balance between work, family and personal living. Twyman is President of Towery Communications, located in Brentwood, Tennessee, just outside of Nashville.

Scott McKain is an author, professional speaker and dog "parent." He travels across the country and around the world speaking on personal and professional development. Scott and his wife, Sheri (along with Keesha and Pepper) live in Indianapolis.

Ann Weeks has been a nurse family therapist in private practice for over 21 years, a former dean of nursing and professional speaker on healing strategies. She has authored 4 books, an audio cassette and video. She has three children, 3 step-children, 4 children's' spouses, 1 dog, 1 cat, 3 granddogs and 6 grandcats!

Stephen Yarnell is a cardiologist, clown, speaker, writer and ex-runner. Lynn is an ultra-runner (100 mile trail run). Mele may miss the ducks but now has bonded to a flop-eared rabbit!

Joe and Helen Hesketh present programs that focus on improving our world by revitalizing relationship at home and in the workplace. Members of the National Speakers Association since 1985. For further information on workshops and keynotes call 206-641-0278 or FAX 206-641-4291.

Mauri Way sells residential real estate in North Dallas. A portion of her proceeds from each transaction are donated to medical research and welfare of animals. She is also patenting a pet product in memory of Tiki & Heather. Their Norfolk Terrier puppy, Bailey Dude, is helping. Mauri can be reached at 214-733-9423.

Elaine Kvitka, registered dietitian, author, nutrition educator and professional speaker gives workshops and speeches on Nutrition and Wellness. Formerly with Pritikin Systems, Inc. she is now with **Heartbeat**™, *the lifestyle change program that puts **more life in your years!*** Elaine can be reached at 602-991-8660.

Ann Chadwell Humphries, president of ETICON, Inc. EtiquetteConsultants for Business and Camp Manners lives in Columbia, SC with her handsome husband, Kirk, their sons, Brad, Charlie, Noah and their cat, Eddie (get it, Eddie-cat?).

Gene Swidell is President of Creative Concepts International, Inc. in Atlanta, GA specializing in business consulting and customized training. He delivers seminars and speeches on management, team building, and customer service. For more information call 404-303-9066.

Rosita Perez is a woman who lives what she speaks, sings and writes. She captivates audiences with vigor, music, outrageous humor and unforgettable honesty. Rosita was designated Speaker of the Year by the National Management Association and has been honored with the Cavett Award by the National Speakers Association.

Mary Pennington and her husband Randy stay busy operating their consulting and training company, Pennington Group Inc., and raising the brother & sister team - Spencer and Katie (poodles of course!).

Paul O. Radde, Ph.D., is a psychologist, and professional speaker. An expert on "Thriving", he keynotes conferences and coaches individuals on the highest life style. He can be reached at 800-966-8333.

Judy Tatelbaum, MSW, is a professional speaker, psychotherapist, and author of books, *The Courage to Grieve* and *You Don't Have to Suffer* published by Harper Collins. For information on her lectures, books, or tapes write PO Box 601, Carmel Valley, CA 93924.

Terri Horvath, Indianapolis, Indiana based writer, photographer and author of *Spread the Word: How to promote nonprofit groups with a network of speakers.*. Terri can be contacted at http://www.the-resource,resource.com/sprdword.html.

Margot Robinson is a management consultant, author of two books, trainer and speaker. She lives in rural North Carolina with her husband Steve Planson and Lulu, mouse, Lucy, Bede (cats) and of course Moon (dog). You can contact her at 910-951-1234(v), 910-951-9966(f), pathways @vnet.net.

Paula Wigboldy is wife of Ken, mother of Kyle, Crystal and Kimberly, Trainer of Jumper, National Coordinator for Sue Hershkowitz, CSP, President of Phoenix Christian School Board and Grand Poo Bah of anyone that asks!

Dick Caldwell (800-387-6301) is a professional speaker and ministerial student. He, Linda, Bubba and Buster now live on a desert acreage in Southern Nevada and are looking for another "TootieDog".

Tom Antion is an entertaining business speaker and professional practical joker. You can reach him and Freeway at 800-448-6280.

Lynn Lively is a Seattle-based professional speaker on workplace decision-making and clear-thinking skills. Lynn reports Scanner, now seven years old, has trained her "bosses" to jog and feed her at 5pm!

Dr. Terry Paulson, from Agoura Hills, CA, is a psychologist, author and speaker on *making change work.* Some of the humor and the energy that brought *Business Digest* to call him "the Will Rogers of management consultants" comes from running and playing soccer with his three-year old Dalmatian, *Sunshine.*

Chris Hanse Baughman is Vice-President in charge of sales for Hanse Environmental, Inc., a test chamber company and President of Hanse Technology, Inc., a seminar company. The mother of 6 children and 2 grandchildren, she still relies on her animals to help.

Kathy Beth Macdonald. The daughter of a US diplomat, Kathy Beth was raised in six different countries (including the United States). She currently lives in Austin, Texas with her husband, Garry, her dog, Heather, and her cat, Robin.

Gail Wenos, CSP, CPAE is a Humorist who travels nation-wide speaking on Teamwork and Making a Difference. She is <u>much</u> more skilled at speaking than she is a training dogs! Gail can be reached at 2626 "B" N. Tustin Ave., Santa Ana, CA 92705 or 714-771-1166.

Dana Murphy is the Vice President of the International Assn. for Exposition Management in Dallas, TX. After her career in association management ends; (5 years or so) she will be moving to Jackson Hole, WY and opening a dog kennel breeding and training Newfoundlands.

Doc Blakely, CSP, CPAE is a professional speaker/humor-ist/writer. For information on his availability, books or tapes, e-mail DocBlakely@AOL.com or call 800-346-3831.

Terryl Bechtol, CSP. T. Bubba Bechtol is a well known co-median in the Country Music Industry and a CSP with the National Speakers Association. He is a funny man with a serious message!

Allen Klein. Allen's mother is very proud of him. "Mr. Jollytologist" is a recipient of a Toastmaster's Award and a Certified Speaking Professional designation from the National Speakers Association. He is author of three best-sell-ing books, *The Healing Power of Humor, Quotations to Cheer You Up When the World is Getting You Down* and *Wing Tips*. Contact him at 1034 Page Street, San Francisco, CA 94117. Phone: 415-431-1913. Fax: 415-431-8600.

Nancy Hershkowitz. Nancy Hershkowitz is a freelance journalist living in Fort Lauderdale, FL. Her current dog, Duncan, is a parti-colored Cocker Spaniel who models on a doggy calendar. Her recent projects include producing a documentary on animal abuse, attending her sons' graduations — Kory from college and Matthew from law school and finally, earning her own bachelor's degree.

Jodi Rudick-Stein Gizmo's mommy, is president of the Advisors Marketing Group, a 36 year old promotional products Co. with three US offices. Jodi is also a high voltage/ high content customer service and marketing speaker, trainer and consultant. Jodi is the national speaker of the year for the promotional products association. (619) 721-3737.

Ida Morrison. Ida Morrison is the mother of three children and seven grandchildren. Gentle and loving, Ida is Sue Hershkowitz' designated, and special, "Aunt."

David Kliman, CMP-Director, Travel Management & Corporate Events Fireman's Fund Insurance Company, Novato, CA. Casey Jones-Expert Golden Retriever and Frisbee Player.

Patricia Ball, CSP, CPAE is the master of Heather, the Sheltie. Patricia is a Certified Speaking Professional, Communications Specialist, Diversity Trainer and Presentation Skills Coach. She is 1995-96 President-Elect of the National Speakers Association and its 1996-97 President.

Ron Dentinger is a comedian on the banquet circuit. He has been clocked at 6 laughs a minute over his 30 minute routine. PO Box 151, Dodgeville, WI 53533. Phone: 608-935-2417

Larry Winget is a business humorist and author of fourteen books. He speaks and writes on the subjects of Teambuilding, Customer Service, Sales, and Prosperity. For information on his speaking or other unique personal development products contact Win Seminars!, PO Box 700485, Tulsa, OK 74170 or call 800-749-4597.

Jim Weems is a former staff member of three different Governor's of Oklahoma. After leaving the political scene Jim became an advertising executive in Tulsa, Oklahoma and eventually started his own graphic design company. Jim designed this book and works with several members of the National Speakers Association.

Ruth Guzley. Dottie shares her home with Ruth Guzley who is an assistant professor at California State University in Chico, CA. She guards their home from strangers and cats, takes naps on a plush couch, loves playing hide-and-seek, and constantly complains about what a tough life she has!

Jeff Blackman is an international speaker, author, broadcaster, lawyer and practical joker...who lives in Glenview, IL. 708-998-0688.

Arnold "Nick" Carter is Vice President, Communications Research, for Nightingale-Conant...and a speaker, author, narrator who's ready to tell you about how dogs are really angels...and, the best medicine!

Rick Kiburz. Chesty was so well known around ASU that if you meet someone who was in the Greek system during this time frame odds are very good they'll know who he was. And they might even have a story!

Sherrie K. Evenson, an exercise Physiologist, recently moved to Portland, OR, with her husband and 3 yr. old daughter. The summer before leaving Ellie's place of rest she was heart warmed by two families of Juncos raised outside the front door in a hanging fuschia plant. Both embedded nests were clearly lined with Ellie's hair.

How do I Order Copies of
Dog Tales for the Heart
for my Friends, Relatives and Colleagues???

To order additional copies of *Dog Tales for the Heart*,
please enclose $12.95, plus $3.00 postage
and mail to:

High Impact Publications
14826 N. 54th Place
Scottsdale, AZ 85254

Other books by Sue A. Hershkowitz

Only the Best on Success .... ($11.95 + $3.00 postage)
> A compilation of Success stories to motivate and inspire you to reach greater personal and professional success

Power Sales Writing .... ($15.95 + $3.00 postage)
> A must for every professional sales person! Discover the secrets to powerful, persuasive writing (even if you prefer torture to writing business letters, proposals and reports!).

We will be happy to pay postage on orders of two or more books!

Dog Tales for the Heart makes the Perfect Gift for all occasions!
Your dog-lover friends will appreciate your thoughtfulness!